Objective-C Memory Management Essentials

Learn and put into practice various memory management techniques in Objective-C to create robust iOS applications

Gibson Tang

Maxim Vasilkov

PUBLISHING

BIRMINGHAM - MUMBAI

Objective-C Memory Management Essentials

First published: March 2015

Production reference: 1190315

Published by Packt Publishing Ltd.
Livery Place
35 Livery Street
Birmingham B3 2PB, UK.

ISBN 978-1-84969-712-5

www.packtpub.com

Credits

Authors
Gibson Tang

Maxim Vasilkov

Reviewers
Emil Atanasov

Christine M. Gerpheide

Commissioning Editor
James Jones

Acquisition Editor
James Jones

Content Development Editor
Amey Varangaonkar

Technical Editor
Vijin Boricha

Copy Editor
Janbal Dharmaraj

Project Coordinator
Leena Purkait

Proofreaders
Simran Bhogal

Maria Gould

Indexer
Hemangini Bari

Graphics
Sheetal Aute

Production Coordinator
Melwyn D'sa

Cover Work
Melwyn D'sa

About the Authors

Gibson Tang grew up loving technology after getting his hands on an old Apple II when he was still a young kid. Since then, he has never stopped keeping pace with technology, and after he coded his first "Hello World" program, he has been hooked on programming ever since.

Following his studies at Nanyang Polytechnic and Singapore Institute of Management and serving a 6-year stint in the Republic of Singapore Navy (RSN), he honed his development skills creating software and games for Yahoo! and other Fortune 500 companies. In 2010, he founded Azukisoft Pte Ltd in Singapore to focus on mobile application development. Since then, he has developed countless mobile applications and games for start-ups and big companies both in USA and Singapore.

Apart from programming, he indulges in various hobbies such as soccer, computer games, and jogging in order to get his regular dose of Vitamin D and to see the sun once in a while. Occasionally, he would be on Steam or `Battle.net` blowing off some steam by slaying monsters and killer robots after a day of programming.

I would like to thank the many people who have contributed to my knowledge of programming over the years. Some honorable mentions go out to the geeks and nerds of `Hackerspace.sg` as they have kept me in stitches with their geek jokes and anime. Next, a great thank you goes to Mugunth Kumar, who is an overflowing fountain of knowledge of all things related to Objective-C. Also, thanks to Subhransu Behera, the organizer of the iOS Dev Scout meetup group in Singapore and finally, to my colleagues at Azukisoft Pte Ltd, namely Igor and Dimitry, who have never failed to amaze me with all their new knowledge and things they have learned over the course of their work with me.

Maxim Vasilkov is a mobile software developer in Azukisoft Pte Ltd. He started programming over 10 years ago. He started with iOS when the SDK was made publicly available, and from that time onwards, he developed a passion for making mobile apps. He is also experienced with other programming languages and has expertise working with various team sizes, which gave him the opportunity to look at different approaches to programming. Outside of work, he is a proud father of beautiful triplets, Anna, Maria, and Victoria, who are now 4 years old. This has helped him try out mobile games for kids and enables him to be an expert in mobile games for kids.

I would like to dedicate this chapter to my lovely wife, Irina, and my three princesses, Anna, Maria, and Victoria. Last but not least, I'd like to thank my colleagues at Azukisoft Pte Ltd and Gibson Tang for giving me an opportunity to work on a lot of challenging projects.

About the Reviewers

Emil Atanasov is an IT consultant who has strong experience with mobile technologies. He is doing his MSc at RWTH Aachen University, Germany. He has worked for several huge USA companies and has been a freelancer for years. He has experience in software design and development, and personally, he has worked on the improvement of many mobile apps. At the moment, he is focused on the rapidly developing mobile sector.

As an Android team leader and senior developer, Emil was leading a team that was developing a part of the Nook Color firmware. This was an e-magazine/e-book reader, which supports the proprietary Barnes & Nobel and many other e-book formats.

Many of the apps that Emil has designed are using Flurry API to track different users' statistics. Based on this experience, he is one of the people behind the *Getting Started with Flurry Analytics* book.

I want to thank my family and friends for being so cool. Thank you for supporting me even though I'm such a bizarre person, who is investing so much of his time in the computer world. Thank you, guys!

Christine M. Gerpheide is a software development engineer at Amazon Web Services. She completed her master's in computer science and engineering with honors from Eindhoven University of Technology in the Netherlands, before which she worked in Greece as a web developer. During her career, Christine has worked on a wide range of software, including service-oriented architectures, model-driven engineering, and mobile development. During her free time, she hikes, runs, and plays violin. Other books reviewed by Christine include *TYPO3 Templates* by Packt Publishing, and she has presented at a number of scientific and open source conferences.

www.PacktPub.com

Support files, eBooks, discount offers, and more

For support files and downloads related to your book, please visit www.PacktPub.com.

Did you know that Packt offers eBook versions of every book published, with PDF and ePub files available? You can upgrade to the eBook version at www.PacktPub.com and as a print book customer, you are entitled to a discount on the eBook copy. Get in touch with us at service@packtpub.com for more details.

At www.PacktPub.com, you can also read a collection of free technical articles, sign up for a range of free newsletters and receive exclusive discounts and offers on Packt books and eBooks.

https://www2.packtpub.com/books/subscription/packtlib

Do you need instant solutions to your IT questions? PacktLib is Packt's online digital book library. Here, you can search, access, and read Packt's entire library of books.

Why subscribe?

- Fully searchable across every book published by Packt
- Copy and paste, print, and bookmark content
- On demand and accessible via a web browser

Free access for Packt account holders

If you have an account with Packt at www.PacktPub.com, you can use this to access PacktLib today and view 9 entirely free books. Simply use your login credentials for immediate access.

Table of Contents

Preface

Managing memory is one of the toughest problems we deal with in Objective-C. This book will provide you with the most important information about effective memory management in your applications.

The practical element will also ensure that the programmers can actively learn key methods and concepts of memory management in a more engaging way rather than just simply read the book. Throughout this book, I will be giving examples of code.

These example code will demonstrate the fundamentals of programming and memory management as well as cover some aspects of iOS development such as Core Data. All these Xcode projects are ready to run out of the box and you do not need any additional setup to run the code. Just make sure that you have the the latest version of Xcode, which is version 6 at this point in time.

So, this book will help you become aware of memory management and how to implement this correctly and effectively while being aware of the benefits at the same time. This tutorial-based book will actively demonstrate techniques for the implementation of memory management, showing the resultant effects on performance and effective implementation.

I have to mention that in this book, I will speak about the most recent standard of Objective-C and Objective-C 2.0. Apple suggests Objective-C as a main tool of development for their platform and strives to improve the product continuously.

I must say that not all of Apple's attempts to improve Objective-C have been entirely successful. Garbage collection is an example of ineffective memory management. It is deprecated since OS X Version 10.8 in favor of Automatic Reference Counting (ARC) and is scheduled to be removed in a future version of OS X.

I have been working with Objective-C for years and C++ for even longer. Hence, memory management is not an alien concept to me as I have been debugging and tracing memory leaks for years in the course of my work at Azukisoft Pte Ltd.

At my job at Azukisoft Pte Ltd, I work mostly with Objective-C but with the occasional C++ thrown into the mix. And this is a very interesting combination, which will be highlighted in this book too.

What this book covers

Chapter 1, Introduction to Objective-C Memory Management, will introduce you to reference counting, Manual Retain Release (MRR), object ownership, sand life cycle, and memory leaks.

Chapter 2, Automatic Reference Counting, will introduce you to ARC and how it works, its advantages, and how to set up your projects to use ARC, memory models in Objective-C, and UIKit with ARC.

Chapter 3, Using Autorelease Pools, introduces you to autorelease pools, autorelease pools mechanics, Apple-autoreleased classes overview, ARC and autorelease, and blocks and threads.

Chapter 4, Object Creation and Storage, will cover the different ways to create objects; a comparison of different memory management options: ARC, MRC, autorelease pools, garbage collection, memory models; and how @property makes your life easier.

Chapter 5, Managing Your Application Data, will cover disk cache, UI techniques of partial data display, serialization and archiving objects, methods to encode and decode objects, cases when you need SQLite, and SQLite versus Core Data.

Chapter 6, Using Core Data for Persistence, explains what Core Data is and why you should use it, NSManagedObject and its use in your application, memory management when using Core Data, and the common errors.

Chapter 7, Key-value Programming Approaches, explains what key-value coding or KVC is, the NSKeyValueCoding protocol, manual subsets of NSKeyValueCoding behavior, associated objects, selectors as keys, maximum flexibility, and handling keys/values.

Chapter 8, Introduction to Swift, highlights Cocoa binding in OS X, differences between automatic and manual key-value observing, and how key-value observation is implemented.

Chapter 9, Memory Management and Debugging, covers memory overuse, collecting data on your app, how to use instruments in Xcode, using the LLVM/Clang Static Analyzer, using NSZombie to help find an over-released object, and plumbing leaks.

Chapter 10, Tips and Tricks for Memory Management, explains the use of accessor methods, declaring accessors using properties, performance guidelines, and when you should avoid KVC and KVO.

Chapter 11, Features of Xcode 6, introduces you to new tools such as view hierarchy debugger, preview editor, and the addition of new functionalities such as allowing storyboards and NIBs to be used as launch images for your application instead of just static images.

What you need for this book

For this book, you will need Apple's Intel-based Macbook, iMac or Mac mini, 2010 models or higher with Xcode installed, version 4.3 or later (which is available at the Mac Apple Store).

Who this book is for

This book is especially designed for developers with minimum experience in Objective-C or another object-oriented programming language as well as tech students with minimum knowledge of programming logic, object-oriented programming, and the Apple OS X environment.

Conventions

In this book, you will find a number of text styles that distinguish between different kinds of information. Here are some examples of these styles and an explanation of their meaning.

Code words in text, database table names, folder names, filenames, file extensions, pathnames, dummy URLs, user input, and Twitter handles are shown as follows: "When you do a new, malloc, or alloc, what the operating system does is that it is giving your program a chunk of memory on the heap."

A block of code is set as follows:

```
int main(int argc, char *argv[]) {

 SomeObject *myOwnObject;
 // myOwnObject is created in main
  myOwnObject = [[SomeObject alloc] init];

   // myOwnObject can be used by other objects
  [anotherObject using:myOwnObject];
```

New terms and **important words** are shown in bold. Words that you see on the screen, for example, in menus or dialog boxes, appear in the text like this: "In Xcode, go to the target **Build Phases** tab, open the **Compile Sources** group, and you will be able to see the source file list."

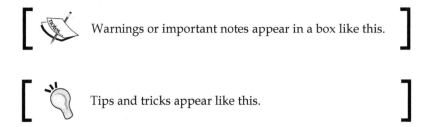

Warnings or important notes appear in a box like this.

Tips and tricks appear like this.

Reader feedback

Feedback from our readers is always welcome. Let us know what you think about this book—what you liked or disliked. Reader feedback is important for us as it helps us develop titles that you will really get the most out of.

To send us general feedback, simply e-mail feedback@packtpub.com, and mention the book's title in the subject of your message.

If there is a topic that you have expertise in and you are interested in either writing or contributing to a book, see our author guide at www.packtpub.com/authors.

Customer support

Now that you are the proud owner of a Packt book, we have a number of things to help you to get the most from your purchase.

Downloading the example code

You can download the example code files from your account at http://www.packtpub.com for all the Packt Publishing books you have purchased. If you purchased this book elsewhere, you can visit http://www.packtpub.com/support and register to have the files e-mailed directly to you.

Errata

Although we have taken every care to ensure the accuracy of our content, mistakes do happen. If you find a mistake in one of our books—maybe a mistake in the text or the code—we would be grateful if you could report this to us. By doing so, you can save other readers from frustration and help us improve subsequent versions of this book. If you find any errata, please report them by visiting http://www.packtpub.com/submit-errata, selecting your book, clicking on the **Errata Submission Form** link, and entering the details of your errata. Once your errata are verified, your submission will be accepted and the errata will be uploaded to our website or added to any list of existing errata under the Errata section of that title.

To view the previously submitted errata, go to https://www.packtpub.com/books/content/support and enter the name of the book in the search field. The required information will appear under the **Errata** section.

Piracy

Piracy of copyrighted material on the Internet is an ongoing problem across all media. At Packt, we take the protection of our copyright and licenses very seriously. If you come across any illegal copies of our works in any form on the Internet, please provide us with the location address or website name immediately so that we can pursue a remedy.

Please contact us at copyright@packtpub.com with a link to the suspected pirated material.

We appreciate your help in protecting our authors and our ability to bring you valuable content.

Questions

If you have a problem with any aspect of this book, you can contact us at questions@packtpub.com, and we will do our best to address the problem.

1
Introduction to Objective-C Memory Management

In this chapter, we will concern ourselves principally with the core issues of the memory management problem as well as an Objective-C-based solution of it. We will look at the ownership and life cycle of the object. This basic idea is known as manual references counting, or **Manual Retain Release** (**MRR**), where you need to claim and relinquish ownership of every object. It defines an object's life cycle. And finally, we'll take a look deeper into **NSObject** for a better understanding of what's going on.

We will cover the following topics in this chapter:

- Why do we need memory management in Objective-C?
- An object's ownership and life cycle
- The principles of reference counting
- What's a memory leak and why pay attention to it?

Why do we need memory management in Objective-C?

It does not matter what programming language is being used; the question of memory management always persists. In general, it is a question of resource management that cannot be avoided because memory is always a limited resource.

The scripting languages and Java, where memory management is handled by the virtual machine or application (where it is hidden from the code), are not always effective enough. While it is easier for the programmer this way, it can have a negative impact on resources, since you don't have an absolute control of it and there are objects still "living" when we don't need them anymore, plus these "living" objects still occupy precious memory space, which can be used by other objects. Additionally, depending on what you ask, another opinion is that an automatic memory management is the only right way to go.

Such talks usually start discussions like "Which is the best programming language?" and" What is the best way of memory management?". Let's leave that meaningless business for blogs' and forums' "Holy-Wars". Every tool has it's use in the correct context and Objective-C memory management concept is quite efficient in terms of both time cost savings and resource saving.

The memory in Objective-C, is managed in a different way from some of the widespread languages such as C/C++, Java, or C#, which are typically taught in schools as it introduces new concepts such as object ownership. Memory management is crucial for devices that run on a limited amount of memory such as mobile phones, smart watches, and so on, since effective memory management will allow you to squeeze every ounce of performance needed to run efficiently on these small devices, where memory is scarce on these devices.

An object's ownership and life cycle

The idea of object ownership abstraction is simple—one entity is simply responsible for another and an entity has the ability to own an object. When an entity owns an object, the entity is responsible to free that object too.

Let's go to our code example. If an object was created and used in the main function, then the main function is responsible for the object, as the following code listing demonstrates:

```
int main(int argc, char *argv[]) {

  SomeObject *myOwnObject;
  // myOwnObject is created in main
   myOwnObject = [[SomeObject alloc] init];

    // myOwnObject can be used by other objects
  [anotherObject using:myOwnObject];

    // but main is responsible for releasing it
   [myOwnObject release];
```

What makes this concept a bit more complicated is that objects can be owned by
more than one entity. So, an object may be created and owned in the main function
and will also be used by another entity that will claim ownership of the object.

A common situation where you will see multiple object ownership is when you
use arrays. Arrays are indexed lists of objects, and when an object is placed into an
array, the array claims ownership of the object. So, if I create an object in the main
function and then put that object into an array, both the main function and the
array will claim ownership of the object and create a reference to it at the same time.
Ownership and reference are different as an object references another object, which it
does not own and both are responsible for cleaning up the object. The following code
demonstrates this:

```
int main (int argc, char *argv[]) {

   SomeObject *myOwnObject;
   // myOwnObject is created in main
myOwnObject = [[SomeObject alloc] init];

   // myOwnObject can be used by other objects
NSMutableArray *myArray;
   // add my object to myArray
myArray = [[NSMutableArray alloc] initWithObjects:myOwnObject,
nil];

   // main does not need myOwnObject any more
[myOwnObject release];

   // but myOwnObject still is needed inside the array
[anotherObj usingArray: myArray];
```

Just like objects in the real world, Objective-C objects are created; they live, and
then go away when the application is closed. This is how the object life cycle works.
Obviously, arrays have to claim the ownership on the object and prevent it to be
deleted in the release method called in the main function.

However, what is the correct way for the entity to claim its rights on an object that it owns? Let's take a deeper look at the problem.

Ownership of object and reference counting

To indicate the number of owners using objects, those objects are given a reference count.

At the beginning, the reference count of the object is 1. This happens because the function creating the object is going to use that object. When any entity needs to claim an ownership of the object, since that entity is going to access and use that object, it sends a retain message to it and its retain count is incremented by 1. When an entity is finished with the object, it sends the release message to the object and its retain count decrements by 1. As long as this object's reference count is higher than zero, some "things" are using it. When it comes to zero, the object is no longer useful for any of those "things", and it can be safely deallocated.

Let's return to the example with the object owned by an array. Explanations are given in the following code comments and diagram:

```
int main(int argc, char *argv[]) {

    SomeObject *myOwnObject;
    // myOwnObject is created in main
     myOwnObject = [[SomeObject alloc] init];
    // myOwnObject has retain count equal to 1

   // myOwnObject can be used by other objects
   NSMutableArray *myArray;
   // add my object to myArray
   myArray = [[NSMutableArray alloc] initWithObjects:myOwnObject,
   nil];
   //inside myOwnObject got another retain message
   //and now its retain count equal 2

   // main does not need myOwnObject any more
   [myOwnObject release];
   // release decrements retain count
   // and now myOwnObject retain count now is 2-1 = 1

   // but myOwnObject still is needed inside the array
   [anotherObj usingArray: myArray];
```

```
[myArray release];
// on array destruction every object inside array gets release
message

//myOwnObject retain count decreases this time to 0 and
myOwnObject will be deleted together with the array
```

The following diagram illustrates the principle of reference counting:

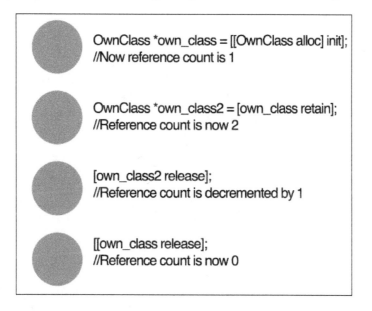

```
OwnClass *own_class = [[OwnClass alloc] init];
//Now reference count is 1


OwnClass *own_class2 = [own_class retain];
//Reference count is now 2


[own_class2 release];
//Reference count is decremented by 1


[[own_class release];
//Reference count is now 0
```

Forgetting to send a release message to an object before setting a pointer to point at something else will guarantee you a memory leak. In order to create an object before it's initiated, a chunk of the OS memory is allocated to store it. Also, if you send a `release` statement to an object, which was not previously sent, a `retain` statement is sent to the object. This will be considered as a **premature deallocation**, where the memory previously allocated to it is not related to it anymore. A lot of time is spent on debugging these issues, which can easily become very complex in large projects. If you don't follow some solid principles for memory management, you can often forget and quickly find yourself getting stuck for hours checking every retain and release statement. Even worse is if you're going through someone else's code, and they mess things up. Going through to fix memory management issues in someone else's code can take forever.

What's a memory leak and why pay attention to it?

A memory leak is when your program loses track of a piece of memory that was allocated and has forgotten to release it. The consequence is that the "leaked" memory will never be freed by the program. When more memory is leaked after a certain point in time, there will be no more free memory and this will cause your application to crash. Usually, this tends to happen when a piece of code does `new`, `malloc`, or `alloc`, but never does a corresponding "delete", "free", or "release" respectively.

When you do `new`, `malloc`, or `alloc`, what the operating system does is that it is giving your program a chunk of memory on the heap. The OS says, "Here, take this memory address and have this block of memory on it." Thus, you need to create a reference to that memory address (usually in the form of a pointer), depending on the OS, such as, "I'm done with this, it's not useful anymore" (by calling "free", "delete", or "release").

Memory leaks happen when you throw away your pointer to that memory. If your program does not retain where your memory is allocated on the heap, how can you even free it? The following line of code shows an example of a memory leak if you never call the release method on it:

```
NSMutableString *str = [[NSMutableString alloc]
initWithString:@"Leaky"];
```

So why should you care? At best, you're the dissipating memory that will be freed when the user quits your app. At worst, there could be a memory leak that happens in every screen. It would not be a great mode to end up your program, especially if the user lets it run for a long time. A program crash is very hard to debug as it can crash at random moments in your application as memory leaks are very unpredictable to replicate and creating an application that crashes often will lead to bad reviews of your program on the App Store, or through word of mouth, which is something that you do not want to happen.

This is why in the process of evolution, there are other methods of memory management in Objective-C, which you will find further in this book.

What is an object within Objective-C?

How do things work inside Objective-C? `NSObject` is the root class of most Objective-C class hierarchies, through it an object inherits basic methods and behaves like an Objective-C object.

This object is an instance of a class and can also be a member of a class or one of its derivatives. So, let's take a deeper look at `NSObject`. In the early stage, Objective-C had a class called `Object`. This had a method called +new, which wrapped `malloc()`, and a method called -free. Since Objective-C objects were generally aliased and managing object life cycles became quite complex, this was troublesome.

NSObject is used by NeXT — Steve Job's second company, founded after he was fired from Apple in 1985 — in order to provide reference counting, thus, dividing Object pointers in two categories: pointers that own references and pointers that do not own references. Those pointers that contribute towards the object's reference count are owning reference pointers. If there is a certainty that a reference is going to be held somewhere else for the duration of a variable's lifetime, a non-owning reference pointer can be used avoiding the additional overhead of reference count manipulation since a non-owning reference pointer does not have the added cost of keeping track of object ownership.

Non-owning reference pointers are often used for autoreleased values. Autorelease pools make it possible for a temporary object to receive a non-owning reference pointer in return. An object, by receiving an -autorelease message is added to a list that will be deallocated afterwards, with the destruction of the current autorelease pool. You can call autorelease using the autorelease method as shown here:

```
[myObject autorelease];
```

The following table shows some description on the roles of autorelease and release:

Release type	Description
The autorelease method	An object is sent a release message, but put in an autorelease pool and the object is released when the pool is drained later during the run loop, but still occupies memory
The release method	An object is released immediately and memory is freed after the object is released

Any object that receives the autorelease message will be released when the autorelease pool is drained. Using autorelease instead of the normal release method will extend the lifetime of an object until the pool is drained at the end of the run loop.

At **Worldwide Developers Conference (WWDC)** 2011, Apple introduced ARC, the acronym of Automatic Reference Counting. It forces the compiler to handle the memory management calls at compile time instead of the conventional garbage collection functionality, which occurs during runtime. ARC also adds some things to the language model in general. It has been supported since iOS5, OS X 10.7, and by GNUstep.

First, what we will find out is that there are two NSObjects in Cocoa, a class and a protocol. Why is this so and what is the purpose of this? Let's look into classes and protocols.

In Objective-C, protocols define a set of behaviors that an object is expected to conform to in certain situations at runtime. For example, a table view object is expected to be able to communicate with a certain data source so that the table view will know what data and information to display. Protocols and classes do not share the same namespaces (a set of identifiers containing names, the names of classes and protocols, thus the same name can exist in different namespaces). It's possible to have both, which are unrelated at the language level, but have the same name. This is the case with NSObject.

If you look at the language, there are no places where you can use either a protocol or a class name. Using class names as the target of message sends, as type names, and in @interface declarations is allowed. Likewise, it's possible to use protocols names in a few identical places; however, not in the same way. Having a protocol with the same name as a class won't result any issue.

It is impossible for root class to have a superclass as they are at the top of the hierarchy, so there is no superclass above a root class and NSObject class is one of them. And I give emphasis on saying *one of them* because in comparison to other programming languages in Objective-C, it's perfectly possible to have the existence of multiple root classes.

Java's single root class is named java.lang.Object, which is the parent ultimate class of any other. For this reason, any piece of code in Java, which comes from any object, has the basic methods added by java.lang.Object.

Cocoa can have multiple root classes. Besides NSObject, there is NSProxy and a few others root classes; and such root classes are, in part, the reason for the existence of the NSObject protocol. The NSObject protocol determines a specific set of basic methods, expecting their implementation by the others root classes, consequently, making those methods available whenever and wherever they are needed.

The NSObject class is in accordance to the NSObject protocol, which results in the implementation of this basic method:

```
//for NSObject class
@interface NSObject <NSObject>
```

Implementing the same method works for NSProxy, which is also in accordance to the NSObject protocol:

```
// for NSProxy class
@interface NSProxy <NSObject>
```

Methods such as hash, description, isEqual, isKindOfClass, isProxy, and others are found in the NSObject protocol. NSProxy to NSObject protocol denotes that, implementing the basic NSObject methods, it's still possible to count on NSProxy instances.

Subclassing NSObject would pull in a lot of baggage that may cause a problem. NSProxy assists in order to prevent this by giving you a simpler superclass that doesn't have so much extra stuff in it.

The fact that the NSObject protocol is useful for root classes isn't all that interesting for most Objective-C programming, for the simple fact that we don't make use of other root classes frequently. However, it will be very convenient when you need to make your own protocols.

Let's say, you have the following protocol:

```
@protocol MyOwnProtocol
- (void)myFunction;
@end
```

And there is a pointer to a simple object, myOwnObject, that accords to it:

```
id<MyProtocol> myOwnObject;
```

You can tell this object to perform myFunction:

```
[myOwnObject myFunction];
```

However, you cannot ask the object for its description:

```
[myOwnObject description]; // no such method in the protocol
```

And you can't check it for equality:

```
[myOwnObject isEqual: anotherObject];
// no such method in the protocol
```

In general, you can't ask it to do any of the stuff that a normal object can do. There are times when this doesn't have any importance, but in some circumstances, you will wish to be able to perform this task.

As mentioned earlier, NSObject, the root class of most Objective-C class hierarchies and through NSObjects, your Objective-C classes can inherit an interface to the system and also gain the ability to behave as Objective-C objects. So, NSObject is important if you want your objects to gain access to methods such as isEqual, so on, and so forth. This is where the NSObject protocol comes into the picture. Protocols can inherit from other protocols, which means that MyProtocol can inherit from the NSObject protocol:

```
@protocol MyOwnProtocol <NSObject>
-  (void)myFunction;
@end
```

This says that not only do objects that conform to MyOwnProtocol respond to myFunction, but they also respond to all those common messages in the NSObject protocol. Knowing that any object in your application directly or indirectly inherits from the NSObject class, that it's in accordance to the NSObject protocol, there is no imposition to any additional requirements on people implementing MyOwnProtocol, while giving you the permission to use these basic methods on instances.

The fact that there are two different NSObjects is abnormal for the frameworks; however, it starts to make sense when you go deeper into it. The NSObject protocol grants the permission to all root classes that have the same basic methods, making, also, a very easy way to declare a protocol that also includes basic functionality expected from any object. The NSObject class introduces it all together, since it's in accordance to the NSObject protocol. One thing to note here is that a custom class that's created and does not inherit NSObject can be considered as a root class, but once you make your custom class inherit from NSObject, then the root class won't be your custom class anymore, and the root class will be NSObject. However, generally, most of your custom classes should inherit from NSObjects; it will implement NSObject's functionality such as alloc, init, release, and so on and without inheriting from NSObject, these functionalities need to be written and implemented by you.

Summary

In this chapter, you learned what memory management in Objective-C is and how it works. You also learned the best practices while working with Manual Retain Release, and got an introduction to Automatic Reference Counting, Objective-C Objects, and root classes. ARC basically can be considered as a compile time guard against memory leaks as the compiler will automatically write the release statements for you at compile time. So, there is no need to write verbose release statements in your code to keep it clean and terse.

One tip to note for coding with memory management is that whenever you do `alloc` and `init`, then write your release code after that and put it in its appropriate place in your class, you can forget to call the release method after writing some or fixing some bugs. So writing your object release statements after you do `alloc` and `init` will help you to keep memory leaks to a minimum so that you won't have a situation where you get a memory leak as you have forgotten to write your object release statement.

In the next chapter, you will learn more about ARC, how it works, its advantages, how to set up your projects to use ARC and memory models in Objective-C and UI Kit with ARC.

2
Automatic Reference Counting

Good ideas live a long life and bad ones die fast. In Objective-C, reference counting's long life was seen as a very good idea. The next step of evolution in this is that it became automatic, so we call it **Automatic Reference Counting (ARC)**, which was introduced by Apple Inc. in 2011 for application development on its desktop and mobile OS, Mac OS X Lion, and iOS 5. It changed the name of the initial referencing counting to **Manual Reference Counting**.

We will cover the following topics in this chapter:

- ARC and how it works
- Advantages and disadvantages of ARC
- Project settings for ARC
- Mixing code that doesn't support ARC with your project
- Memory model in Objective C
- ARC in UI kit

What is ARC and how does it work?

If you remember, the idea of reference counting covers the actual deletion of objects from the memory. With reference counting, Objective-C takes care of the actual object destruction. Owner objects are only responsible for releasing their claim of ownership on the object. So, logically the idea that appeared next was to make everything completely automatic as it was done in languages such as Java and C#. This idea was developed in the Garbage collection branch and Automatic Reference Counting.

Garbage collection is only available for Mac OS X, starting with version 10.5. Also, note that iOS applications can't use Garbage collection; since it relies on the power of the device, it will take some time to process, forcing the user to wait the process end, thus producing a bad user experience. It is also deprecated since OS X Version 10.8 is in favor of ARC and is scheduled to be removed in the forthcoming versions of OS X.

ARC is a new and innovative way that contains many of the Garbage collection's advantages, yet different from Garbage collection. ARC does not have any process in the background to make the object's deallocation, which gives ARC a big advantage against Garbage collection when comparing their performance.

However, before explaining how ARC does this, it's important to understand what ARC does not do:

- ARC does not impose a runtime memory model as Garbage collection does. Code compiled under ARC uses the same memory model as plain C or non-ARC Objective-C code, and can be linked to the same libraries.

- ARC only makes automatic memory management possible for Objective-C objects, inherited from NSObject (note that in Objective-C, blocks also happen to be objects under the covers though).

- Memory allocated in any other way is not touched and must still be managed manually. The same goes for other resources such as file handles and sockets, such as streams.

How ARC looks

Start by picturing a traditional Objective-C source code file written by an expert Cocoa programmer. The retain, release, and autorelease messages are sent in all the right places and are in perfect balance.

Now, imagine editing the source code file, removing every instance of the retain, release, and autorelease messages, and changing a single build setting in Xcode that instructs the compiler to put all the suitable memory management calls back into your program when the source code is compiled. That's ARC. It's just what the name suggests — traditional Cocoa reference counting, being automatically done.

At its core, ARC is not a runtime service; it doesn't work on program execution, as Garbage collection does. On the other hand, the new Clang, the compiler frontend for C, C++, Objective-C, and Objective-C++, provides it as a two-part phase (we will call these phases "cycles"). In the following diagram, you can see these two phases. At the cycle named **frontend** as shown in the following diagram, **Clang** will analyze every preprocessed file for properties and objects. And then, relying on a few fixed rules, it will insert the correct statements — retain, release, and autorelease.

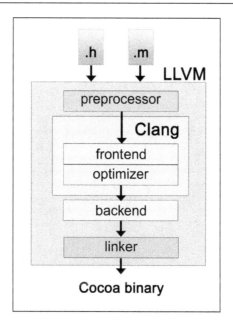

For instance, if an object is allocated and locally corresponds to a method, this object will have a `release` statement close to that method's endpoint. This `release` statement, if it is a class property, comes into the `dealloc` method in a class, which can be your custom class or any Objective-C class. If it's a collection object or a return value, it will get an `autorelease` statement. However, if it was referenced as weak, it will be left in peace.

The frontend also inserts `retain` statements for disowned objects locally. It goes to every declared accessor and updates them with the directive `@property`. It includes calls to the `dealloc` routine of their superclasses such as `NSObject` or `UIViewController` or even your own `customer` superclass. It will also report any explicit management call and double ownership.

In the optimize cycle, the modified sources are sent to load balancing by Clang. So, it calculates the retain and release calls created for each object, and reduces all to the optimal minimum. This action avoids excessive `retain` and `release` messages with the possibility to impact with full performance:

```
To see how it works, take a look at the following code:
@class MyBar;
@interface MyFoo
{
@private
    NSString *myOwnString;
}
```

```
@property(readonly) NSString *myOwnString;

- (MyBar *)getMyBarWithString:(NSString *)myString;
- (MyBar *)getMyBar;

@end


@implementation MyFoo;
@dynamic myOwnString;

- (MyBar *)getMyBarWithString:(NSString *)myString
{
    MyBar *yBar;

    if (![self.myString isEqualToString:myString])
    {
        myOwnString = myString;
    }
    return [self getMyBar];
}

- (MyBar *)getMyBar
{
    MyBar *yBar

    return yBar;
}
@end
```

Now, it's an Objective-C class with no `retain` or `release`. There is one private property named `myOwnString`, which is an instance of `NSString`. This class imports the header of the `MyBar` class (line 1) and declares a read-only getter with the same name, `myOwnString`. There is a modifier called `getMyBarWithString` and an internal function named `getMyBar`.

The following code is the same piece of code using **Manual Reference Counting (MRC)**:

```
@class MyBar;
@interface MyFoo
{
@private
    NSString *myOwnString;
}
```

```objc
@property (readonly) NSString *myOwnString;

- (MyBar *)getMyBarWithString:(NSString *)myString;
- (MyBar *)getMyBar;

@end



@implementation MyFoo;
@dynamic myOwnString;

- (MyBar *)getMyBarWithString:(NSString *)myString
{
    MyBar *yBar;

    if (![self.myString isEqualToString:myString])
    {
        [myString retain];
        [myOwnString release];
        myOwnString = myString;
    }
    return [self getMyBar];
}

- (MyBar *)getMyBar
{
    MyBar *yBar

    [yBar autorelease];
    return yBar;
}

- (void)dealloc
{
    [myOwnString release];
    [super dealloc];
}
@end
```

Note that the class interface is still the same. However, now, the `getMyBarWithString` modifier has some new statements; more specifically, two:

```objc
[myString retain];
[myOwnString release];
```

Sending a release statement to the `myOwnString` property (line 24) is the responsibility of one of them. The other sends a `retain` message to the `myString` argument (line 25). Before returning the last one as its result, the `getMyBar` function sends locally a `autorelease` statement to the `yBar` local. Lastly, MRC supersedes the `dealloc` method of that class. MRC also releases the `myOwnString` property (line 44) and invokes the `dealloc` method of its superclass (line 45); still in that method, if there is already a `dealloc` method, MRC properly updates its code.

When using ARC, you don't need to explicitly insert `retain` and `release` messages, as ARC will automatically insert them during compilation. Since ARC decides by itself how an Objective-C object will be better managed, the time that will be required to develop the class code is not required anymore. So, ARC avoids any empty pointers. ARC can also be excluded on a per-file basis where you select your target, go to **Build Phases,** and add the **-fno-objc-arc** flag in **Compiler Flags**.

However, the Clang compiler is built into LLVM 3.0, only available on Xcode since version 4.2. There has been optimized runtime support for ARC ever since Mac OS X Version 10.7 and iOS Version 5.0. It is not challenging to use ARC with binaries from Mac OS X 10.6 and iOS 4.3, but for iOS 4.3, it's only achievable through blue code; and for OS X 10.6, the newest version does not make use of weak pointers at all.

Some points about ARC are as follows:

- It does not work with `AppleScriptObjC` or even `PyObjC` sources; it works exclusively with Objective-C sources.

- However, more or less, when there are `PyObjC` and `AppleScriptObjC` classes being connected to Cocoa by Objective-C code, ARC will affect that underlying code.

- Note that for some third-party frameworks, if ARC is enabled, they might crash while compiling. Ensure that the developer of such a framework can and will update it.

Project settings for ARC

When a project is set to utilize ARC, the compiler flag `-fobjc-arc` is by default set for every Objective-C source file. ARC can be disabled for particular classes through the compiler flag, `-fno-obj-arc`. In Xcode, go to the target **Build Phases** tab, open the **Compile Sources** group, and you will be able to see the source file list. When you double-click on the file where you want to set it, a pop-up panel will appear. In that panel, get in the `-fno-obj-arc` flag and click on **Done** to finish.

If ARC was not enabled when the project was created, then to enable it, follow this process:

1. Open the project.
2. Go to **Edit | Refactor | Convert to Objective-C ARC**.
3. If there is no problem and it's ready to convert, it will check your code.

By default, all newly created Objective-C projects in Xcode 5 are enabled with ARC. However, if you need to disable it, follow these steps:

1. Select **Project**.
2. Select **Targets**.
3. From the right panel, go to **Build Settings**.
4. Select **Automatic Reference Counting**.
5. Select **Apple LLVM compiler 3.0 – Language**.
6. Locate **Objective-C++ Automatic Reference Counting** and, in all three sections, select **NO**.

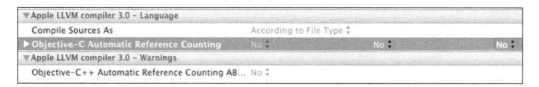

A memory model in Objective-C

A very significant improvement in Objective C 2.0 is its memory model. The countless remnants of problems from the first Objective-C implementations as a preprocessor that induced C were cleaned up. In older versions, Objective-C objects were simply C structures, containing a pointer to their classes in their first fields, and its pointers were just able to receive messages when you wanted to send them.

Now every object pointer comes into one of the following categories: weak, strong, autoreleasing, and unsafe unretained. When ARC is disabled, the programmer is responsible to take care of them all, being sure that they are all safe, for the reason that all those pointers just fit the last category.

The default category (type qualifier) is a strong pointer; they are largely correspondent to the consequences of writing flawless defensive retain/release code. Assigning to a strong pointer is relative to retain the new value and release the old value, because owning references are stored in those pointers.

You need to use `autoreleasing` pointers in order to store values that are autoreleased. In Objective-C, such pointers are the most habitual form of non-owning reference pointers; they are variables on the heap storing autoreleased values. An owning reference pointer, also known as an instance variable, will only be autoreleased when it is stored to a non-owning reference pointer, known as an autoreleasing variable. If you simply store an autoreleased reference pointer, you will have a simple attribution.

In order to decrease the quantity of release and retain statements in a crucial piece of code, it's possible to make use of _autoreleasing, one of the four ARC type qualifiers. However, since the objects will be included in the autoreleasing pool and ARC can commonly eliminate this, it's usually not required to use this type qualifier, besides the fact that is can make things slower.

Weak is the last category (type qualifier) of pointer. If you used the garbage-collector mode in Objective-C, you probably already met `weak` pointers by storing an object in such a pointer. It's not seen as an owning reference pointer (for instance, a variable), and when the object is deallocated, this point is immediately set to nil.

We can count many differences between GC and ARC mode, but the very important one is about ARC being deterministic. It's possible to see it through `weak` pointers. See the following code for an example:

```
id strong = [NSObject new];
__weak id weak = strong;
strong = nil;
NSLog(@"%@", weak);
```

Firstly, since in the garbage collection mode__weak is not granted for on-stack variables, the preceding code won't even pass through compilation. However, what would happen if the weak declaration is moved to somewhere it's valid? We presume that at this point, the object's last reference is already gone. However, the log statement will show you that the object is still there, alive. Relying on the optimizations that the compiler is running, the collector can possibly see its references on the heap if you run the collector by force.

This piece of code will be compiled in the ARC mode — now, weak variables are allowed on the heap.

What you need to know about ARC and weak references

Weak references have been supported on GNUstep Objective-C runtime since version 1.5, since version 5 of iOS, and version 10.7 of OS X. ARC works through the compatibility library as well, but it requires modifications of many classes in order to work with weak references.

Summary

In this chapter, we focused our attention on Automatic Reference Counter, its advantages, how it works, and how to properly set up and integrate it into current projects.

In the next chapter, we will talk about the autorelease pool mechanism and its classes, blocks, and threads. We will also understand the memory model in Objective-C. I hope this chapter has provided you with a good understanding of ARC.

3
Using Autorelease Pools

Consider that you are returning an object you've created (and therefore own) to a caller. If it's released inside your method, the returning object will be an invalid one. On the other hand, there is the basic rule that you have to release the objects you own; then, how do you release them? Simply put the object in the autorelease pool. The object is then released when the autorelease pool is drained.

We will cover the following topics in this chapter:

- Understanding the autorelease pool mechanism
- How autorelease pool helps
- Autoreleased classes
- Autoreleased pool blocks and threads
- Memory model in Objective-C
- ARC with weak references

Understanding the autorelease pool mechanism

When you first start developing for Cocoa (iOS or Mac OS) you quickly learn to follow the standard `alloc`, `init`, and (eventually) `release` cycles:

```
// Allocate and init
NSMutableDictionary *dictionary = [[NSDictionary alloc] init];

// Do something with dictionary
// ...

// Release
[dictionary release];
```

This is great until you discover the convenience of just doing the following:

```
// Allocate and init
NSMutableDictionary *dictionary = [NSDictionary dictionary];

// Do something with dictionary
// …
```

Let's look inside and see what actually happens:

```
NSMutableDictionary *dictionary = [[NSDictionary alloc] init];
return [dictionary autorelease];
```

This approach is called autorelease pools and they are a part of the **Automated Reference Counting (ARC)** memory management model used by the Cocoa platform.

The ARC compiler will autorelease any object for you, unless it's returned from a method that starts with new, alloc, init, copy, or mutableCopy in its name. As before, these objects are placed into an autorelease pool, but in order to introduce a new language construct, NSAutoreleasePool has been replaced by @ autoreleasepool, a compiler directive. Even using ARC, we are still free to use autorelease messages to drain/create our pool at any time. It doesn't affect the compiler when implementing retain and release messages, but provides hints when it's safe to make autoreleased objects go out of scope.

Cocoa frameworks (Foundation Kit, Application Kit, and Core Data) have some suitable methods to handle basic classes that inherit from NSObject, as NSString, NSArray, NSDictionary, and many more. These methods quickly allocate, initialize, and return the created object for you, which will also be autoreleased without you worrying about it so much.

 Note that I really meant "without worrying so much", not "without worrying at all" because even with these handy frameworks that create and clear the object for you, there will be cases when you want to take more control and create additional autorelease pools yourself.

Basically, an autorelease pool stores objects and when it's drained, it just sends the object a release message. The NSAutoreleasePool class is used to support Cocoa's reference-counted memory management system.

Autorelease pools were made by Apple and have been part of the language itself since OS X 10.7. If a program references the NSAutoreleasePool class while in ARC mode, it's considered invalid and is rejected in the build phase. Instead, in ARC mode, you need to replace it with @autoreleasepool blocks, thus defining a region where an autorelease pool is valid, as you can see in the following code:

```
// Code in non-ARC mode
NSAutoreleasePool *myPool = [[NSAutoreleasePool alloc] init];
// Taking advantage of a local autorelease pool.
[myPool release];
```

In ARC mode, however, you should write:

```
@autoreleasepool {
    // Taking advantage of a local autorelease pool.
}
```

Even if you don't use ARC, you can take advantage of @autoreleasepool blocks that are far more effective than the NSAutoreleasePool class.

Opposite to an environment that uses garbage collection, in one with reference counting, every object that receives an autorelease message is placed into an NSAutoreleasePool object. This NSAutoreleasePool class is like a collection of these objects and goes one by one sending a release message when it's drained. It drains the pool when you're out of scope. Then, every object retain's count is decreased by 1. By using an autorelease as an alternative to a release message, you extend the object's lifetime, this time maybe even longer if the object is later retained or at least until the NSAutoreleasePool class is drained. If you put an object into the same pool more than once, for each time, it will receive a release message.

While into an environment with reference counting, Cocoa presumes there will always be an autorelease pool available; otherwise, objects that have received an autorelease message won't get released. This practice will leak memory and generate proper warning messages.

At the beginning of a cycle of the event loop, an autorelease pool is created by the Application Kit (one of the Cocoa frameworks, also known as AppKit). It provides code to create and interact with GUI, and it's drained at the end of this cycle, then every autoreleased object created when processing an event is just released. It means you don't need to create the pools yourself as the Application Kit does it for you. However, if there are many autoreleased objects created by your application, you should consider the creation of "local" autorelease pools; this is an advantage to avoid the peak memory footprint.

To create an NSAutoreleasePool object, you can use the regular alloc and init methods and use drain to dismiss it. A pool cannot be retained; the consequences of drain is like a deallocation, and it's very important to do so in the same context you created it.

Every thread has its own stack of autorelease pools. These stacks contain NSAutoreleasePool objects, which in turn contain autoreleased objects. Every new autoreleased object is placed on the top of the pool and every new pool is placed on the top of the stack. A pool is removed from a stack when it's drained. Before a thread is finished, it drains every autorelease pool on its stack. Despite the fact that an autorelease pool can be manually created and objects can be manually added to it, ARC still drains the pool automatically: you're not allowed to do it yourself.

To ensure that you don't have to worry about ownership, this is what ARC does: easily create autorelease pools, and make them temporarily handle the holding and releasing of autoreleased objects for you.

Autorelease pool mechanism

There will be times when you need to renounce an object's ownership and a good way to do it is by using autorelease pool blocks. Those blocks provide a mechanism where you can renounce it and avoid any chance of the object's immediate deallocation. Even if sometimes you will need to create your own blocks, or it will be in your advantage to do this way, you normally don't need to create them, but there are situations where you may need it.

As in the following code, an autorelease pool block is marked by the usage of @ autoreleasepool:

```
@autoreleasepool {
    //-----
    // Here you create autoreleased objects.
    //-----
}
```

Objects that were created inside the block receive a release message when the block is terminated. An object receives release messages as many times as it receives an autorelease message inside the block.

Autorelease pool blocks can be nested as well:

```
@autoreleasepool {
    // . . .
    @autoreleasepool {
        // . . .
```

```
        }
        //. . .
    }
```

If an autorelease message is not sent inside the autorelease pool block, Cocoa will return error messages and your application will leak memory. You generally don't need to create your own autorelease pool blocks, but there are three situations where you will be required to:

- While creating a program that is not based on UI, such as a command-line one
- While creating a loop that generates a large number of temporary objects
- When a secondary thread has to be created

Reducing peak memory footprint with autorelease pool blocks

Memory footprint is basically the primary amount of memory used by a program in runtime. Temporary autoreleased objects are created in countless applications, and they add to the application's memory footprint until the block is ended. Allowing this accumulation until the current event loop finally ends, in some cases, may result in an exorbitant overhead and you might want to quickly get rid of those temporary objects; after all, they are highly adding to the memory footprint. In this case, the creation of your own "local" autorelease pool blocks is a solution. In the end, all objects are released, consequently deallocated, beneficially reducing the memory footprint.

Here, you can see how to use an autorelease pool block for a `for` loop:

```
NSArray *myUrls = <# Sample Array of URLs #>;
for (NSURL *url in myUrls) {
    @autoreleasepool {

/* Two objects are created inside this pool:
NSString "contents", NSError "error"
At the end of the pool, they are released. */

        NSError *error;
        NSString *contents = [NSString
          stringWithContentsOfURL:url
          encoding:NSUTF8StringEncoding error:&error];

        /* Here you can process the NSString contents,
    thus creating and autoreleasing more objects. */
        }
    }
```

There is NSArray with many files' URLs and the loop processes one file at a time. Every object created inside the block is released when it's ended.

Every object that was autoreleased inside the autorelease pool block is considered disposed of after the block's termination. If you want to keep a temporary object and use it after the autorelease pool block is ended, you must do two things: inside the block, send a retain message to that object and then, only after the block, send the autorelease message, as we can see in the following code sample:

```
- (id)findTheMatchingObject:(id)myObject {

    id myMatch;
    while (myMatch == nil) {
    @autoreleasepool {

    /*
        This search creates a large number of temporary
        objects
    */
            myMatch = [self expensiveSearchForObject:myObject];

            if (myMatch != nil) {
        /*
        Keep myMatch in order to use it even after the block is
        ended.
        */
        [myMatch retain];
        break;
            }
        }
    }
     /*
        Here - outside the block - you send it an
        autorelease message and return it to the method's invoker
    */
    return [myMatch autorelease];
}
```

As the comments in the preceding code explain, by sending a retain message to myMatch inside the autorelease pool block and then, only after the block, sending it an autorelease message increases this object's lifetime, making it available to receive messages outside and properly return it to the method's invoker.

An overview of Apple autoreleased classes

As it was said before, the Cocoa framework provides factory methods with autorelease for many of the basic classes such as NSString, NSArray, NSDictionary, NSColor, and NSDate. However, in the same time, there are some classes that deserve special attention.

NSRunLoop

While using NSRunLoop, at the beginning of every run loop, an autorelease pool will be created, and it will only be destroyed at the end of this run loop. To clarify, every temporary object created inside it will be deallocated at the end of the running iteration. It might not be beneficial if you are creating a large number of temporary objects inside the block; in this case, you should consider creating a new autorelease pool, as shown here:

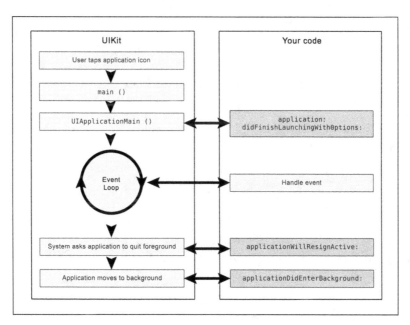

The following code demonstrates what was discussed earlier:

```
id myPool = [NSAutoreleasePool new];
[myObject somethingThatCreatesManyObjects];
[myPool drain];
```

Notice that in order to end the autorelease pool, instead of sending a `release` message, we sent a `drain` message. It was done this way because in garbage collector mode, Objective-C runtime will simply ignore `release` messages, while the `drain` message won't be ignored, providing a hint to the collector; however, it doesn't destroy the autorelease pool.

Application Kit creates an autorelease pool in the main thread at the beginning of each iteration, event, and releases it at the end of each iteration, thus exempting all autorelease objects created during the processing of the event.

Basically, the run loop in iOS waits for the complete execution of an event until the application does something else. These events can be touchscreen interactions, incoming calls, and so on.

For each iOS event handling, a new autorelease pool is created at the beginning and released (drained) when the event's processing is completed. Theoretically, it can be any number of nested autorelease pools, but remember they are created at the beginning of the event's processing.

NSException

Exceptions may happen, and if they do occur, autorelease pools are automatically cleaned up after them. Autorelease pools prove to be a handful tool in order to write exception-safe code.

Even an exception object itself should be autoreleased:

```
// This exception will be autoreleased
+[NSException exceptionWithName:...]

// Or the alternative below
+[NSException raise:...]
```

Using one of the preceding patterns will properly free the memory if an exception is thrown. It will free the memory in garbage collector mode as well, even if it's not required in this GC mode:

```
id myObj = [[[SampleClass alloc] init] autorelease];
ThisMightThrowAnException();

id myObj = [[SampleClass alloc] init];
@try {
    ThisMightThrowAnException();
} @finally {
    [myObj release];
}
```

ARC and autorelease

ARC does still use autorelease as a mechanism, but besides that, its compiled code is created to interoperate with no problem with MRC compiled code, thus autorelease is present.

Despite the fact that ARC does a good job handling the memory management for us, there is still a situation when you need to use autorelease. Sometimes, we create a large number of temporary objects and many of them are only used once. In this case, you might want to free up the memory used by them.

In order to dealloc those objects into the autorelease pool instead of waiting for them to be freed naturally, check out the following code sample in a non-ARC environment:

```
/*
 ---------------------------------------------------------
 Non-ARC Environment with Memory Leaks
*/
@autoreleasepool
{
  // No autorelease call here
   MyObject *obj = [[MyObject alloc] init];

   /* Since MyObject is never released its
      a leak even when the pool exits
   */
}

 /*
  ---------------------------------------------------------
  Non-ARC Environment with NO Memory Leaks
*/
@autoreleasepool
{
   // Memory is freed once the block ends
   MyObject *obj = [[[MyObject alloc] init] autorelease];
}
```

The following sample code is for an ARC environment:

```
/*
 ---------------------------------------------------------
 ARC Environment
*/
@autoreleasepool
```

```
{

    MyObject *obj = [[MyObject alloc] init];
  /*
     No need to do anything once the obj variable
     is out of scope. There are no strong pointers
     so the memory will be free
  */


}

/*
  --------------------------------------------------------
  ARC Environment
*/
MyObject *obj; // Strong pointer from elsewhere in scope

@autoreleasepool
{
    obj = [[MyObject alloc] init];
    // Not freed still has a strong pointer
}
```

Autorelease pool blocks and threads

You will need to create your own autorelease pool if you are making Cocoa calls outside the main thread of the Application Kit. It may happen that you create a foundation-only application for example, or separate a thread.

If your application generates a large number of autoreleased objects, instead of maintaining a single autorelease pool, you are highly advised to drain the autorelease pool and create a new one frequently. This behavior is used by Application Kit on the main thread. If you neglect this, your autoreleased objects don't deallocate, growing the memory footprint. On the other hand, if your thread doesn't make Cocoa calls, you can easily ignore this advice.

Summary

In this chapter, we reviewed autorelease pools and how to properly use them. We also highlighted the differences between NSAutoreleasePool and the new @autoreleasepool classes and its benefits.

In the next chapter, we will talk about a few concepts related to object creation and initialization, such as immutability, inheritance, and so on. We will delve into design patterns such as singletons, which are commonly used in the iOS SDK, such as the UIApplication class that has a method called sharedApplication. We will also look into properties as a way to define the information that a class intends to encapsulate. We will also look into custom methods and format specifiers in *Chapter 4, Object Creation and Storage*. We will cover a lot of materials in the next chapter, so sit tight and hang on while we head to *Chapter 4, Object Creation and Storage*!

Object Creation and Storage

In this chapter, we will cover objects and classes in more depth, showing the mechanisms behind their creation, handling, and customization.

We will cover the following topics:

- Object creation and initialization
- Object immutability
- Object mutability
- Object inheritance
- Convenience initializers
- The singleton pattern
- Using @property
- Types of classes
- Custom methods
- Format specifiers

Creation and initialization of objects

For a developer, building iOS and OS X applications requires a lot of time in creating and handling objects. In Objective-C, like any other object-oriented programming language, the object acts like a data package with predefined behaviors. We can think about an application as an environment containing objects that connect with each other, passing and receiving information such as how to build a graphical interface, how to proceed with user interactions, how and where to store and take data from, how to perform calculations, and much more. The complexity of tasks that can be performed by an object can be very large, but it's not reflected on the complexity to create an object.

Cocoa (for OS X) and Cocoa Touch (iOS) already provide a library containing an extensive list of objects for you to use as they are or create your own objects based on them — we call it code reuse.

One of the most important development processes is thinking about the app base structure, when you decide which object to use, combine, customize, how they will communicate in order to generate the expected output, and so on. Some of them are provided by Cocoa and Cocoa Touch for immediate use such as NSString, NSArray, NSDictionary, UIView, and UILabel, but such importance is due to others who might need customization to act as required and/or in order to create an unique framework — features for your application.

What is a class?

In object-oriented programming approaches, an object is an instance of a class. The class will determine the behavior of the object, the messages (methods) it receives, and sometimes who has access to send these messages in order to obtain a response.

A class describes the properties and behaviors of a specified object, just like the blueprint of a house will describe the properties of the house, such as the number of doors in the house. Similarly, for a number, an instance of a class named NSNumber, its class provides many ways to obtain, analyze, compare, and convert the object's internal numeric value.

Except the internal contents stored in multiple instances of a class, all the properties and actions behave identically. Check out the following example:

```
/*
    ==============================================
    Our object is created here as instance of
    NSNumber.
    We directly assign a float number to it;
    ==============================================
*/

NSNumber *sampleNumber = @(3.1415);

/*
    ==============================================
    Now, we send the built-in message "intValue"
    to convert the float value stored in it to
    an integer value.
```

```
    ===============================================
*/

    NSNumber firstNumber = @([ sampleNumber intValue]);
```

Our numeric object, `firstNumber`, now has the numeric value 3, which is an integer, after sending the message `intValue`, which is predefined in the `NSNumber` class. The object will behave as expected by converting its value to an integer. Any object instance of the class will act in the same way.

Objects are created to be used in different expected ways, but it's not a requirement for you to know how the internal mechanisms of their behavior happens, which is also known as encapsulation. Instead, the single requirement is to know how to handle the objects in order to behave in the way you want. It means you need to know the predefined messages to send to your object. If you have a string, an instance of the `NSString` class containing six uppercase characters, and you want them to be lowercase, all you have to know is the message to be sent:

```
/*
    ===============================================
    We create our string with the uppercase
    characters: "QWERTY"
    ===============================================
*/

    NSString *sampleString = @"QWERTY";

/*
    ===============================================
    Now, we send a message to it, requesting to
    convert the uppercase characters to lowercase
    ===============================================
*/

    sampleString = [sampleString lowercaseString];

/*
    ===============================================
    After this process, our string has now the
    characters: "qwerty"
    ===============================================
*/
```

To specify how an object is intended to be used, we use the class interface. It defines a public interface to be used in other parts of your code, outside the class itself.

Classes

In order to create your own class, go to **File | New** in the menu bar or just click *Command + N*, select **iOS** or **OS X** based on your project and select **Cocoa Class** or **Cocoa Touch Class**. After this, you can name your class and select its super class (from which it will inherit). Xcode will automatically create a header and an implementation file for you, `.h` and `.m`. As in other programming languages, the header file is kind of a summary, a quick view about the contents in the class, what will be used, and so on.

Your public methods and properties will be declared in the header file. Here, you can see a sample of a newly created header file (`mySpecialTableViewController.h`):

```
1   //
2   //  mySpecialTableViewController.h
3   //  BookSample
4   //
5   //  Created by Maxim Vasilkov on 27/11/14.
6   //  Copyright (c) 2014 Arthur Alves. All rights reserved.
7   //
8
9   #import <UIKit/UIKit.h>
10
11  @interface mySpecialTableViewController : UITableViewController
12
13  @end
14
```

Our class is named `mySpecialTableViewController`, a subclass of `UITableViewController`. It creates a UI element, as its name suggests, a table view, which is very common in iOS applications.

Still in our header file, we will create a public property, `NSArray`, to receive and hold the data that will be shown on each `UITableViewCell`. Our table view will show a list of programming languages:

```
1   //
2   //  mySpecialTableViewController.h
3   //  BookSample
4   //
5   //  Created by Maxim Vasilkov on 27/11/14.
6   //  Copyright (c) 2014 Arthur Alves. All rights reserved.
7   //
8
9   #import <UIKit/UIKit.h>
10
11  @interface mySpecialTableViewController : UITableViewController
12
13  @property (strong, nonatomic) NSArray *myProgrammingLanguages;
14
15  @end
16
```

By specifying the superclass during the creation, Xcode already prepared your class with the built-in methods available/required to run it. As we can see in our implementation file (`mySpecialTableViewController.m`), we just need to implement our code:

```
1   //
2   //  mySpecialTableViewController.m
3   //  BookSample
4   //
5   //  Created by Maxim Vasilkov on 27/11/14.
6   //  Copyright (c) 2014 Arthur Alves. All rights reserved.
7   //
8
9   #import "mySpecialTableViewController.h"
10
11  @interface mySpecialTableViewController ()
12
13  @end
14
15  @implementation mySpecialTableViewController
16
17  - (void)viewDidLoad {
18      [super viewDidLoad];
19
20      // Uncomment the following line to preserve selection between presentations.
21      // self.clearsSelectionOnViewWillAppear = NO;
22
23      // Uncomment the following line to display an Edit button in the navigation bar for this view
                controller.
24      // self.navigationItem.rightBarButtonItem = self.editButtonItem;
25  }
26
27  - (void)didReceiveMemoryWarning {
28      [super didReceiveMemoryWarning];
29      // Dispose of any resources that can be recreated.
30  }
31
32
33  - (NSInteger)numberOfSectionsInTableView:(UITableView *)tableView {
34
35      // Return the number of sections.
36      return 0;
37  }
38
39  - (NSInteger)tableView:(UITableView *)tableView numberOfRowsInSection:(NSInteger)section {
40
41      // Return the number of rows in the section.
42      return 0;
43  }
```

Our table view will be simple, only showing each programming language stored in the `myProgrammingLanguages` array on a different cell. It will only have one section, which means we are free to return this number in the `numberOfSectionsInTableView:` method:

```
33  - (NSInteger)numberOfSectionsInTableView:(UITableView *)tableView {
34
35      // Return the number of sections.
36      //return 0; // Original value
37      return 1; // Our modified value.
38  }
39
```

The next modification is to specify the number of rows, which means the number of cells. If it relies on a property where this number might be different, we can't hardcode it as we did with the number of sections; instead, we return the number of objects our array is holding:

```
39
40   - (NSInteger)tableView:(UITableView *)tableView numberOfRowsInSection:(NSInteger)section {
41
42       // Return the number of rows in the section.
43       //return 0;
44       return [self.myProgrammingLanguages count];
45   }
```

The next step when creating a table view in Objective-C is to set the content of the cells. We use the `tableView:cellForRowAtIndexPath:` method (already provided in the implementation file). By default, it comes commented. Uncomment the method in order to use it:

```
79   - (UITableViewCell *)tableView:(UITableView *)tableView cellForRowAtIndexPath:(NSIndexPath *)
         indexPath {
80       UITableViewCell *cell = [tableView dequeueReusableCellWithIdentifier:@"reuseIdentifier"
             forIndexPath:indexPath];
81
82       // Configure the cell...
83
84       return cell;
85   }
```

The first thing you should notice is that it creates `UITableViewCell` and returns it to be seen on the table view. It is between these two steps that we will configure our cell.

The `UITableViewCell` class already comes with a property called `textLabel`. We will use it to show the values stored in the `myProgrammingLanguages` array. Once the `tableView:numberOfRowsInSection:` method returns the number of elements in the array, for each iteration, it configures and returns a cell for the respective item in the array. The first cell is for the first item, the second cell for second item, and so on. Inside this method, the current cell is already the correct cell for `indexPath`, but in order to get the correct value set to it, we use `indexPath.row` to select the proper item in the array:

```
79   - (UITableViewCell *)tableView:(UITableView *)tableView cellForRowAtIndexPath:(NSIndexPath *)
         indexPath {
80       UITableViewCell *cell = [tableView dequeueReusableCellWithIdentifier:@"reuseIdentifier"
             forIndexPath:indexPath];
81
82       // Configure the cell...
83       cell.textLabel.text = self.myProgrammingLanguages[indexPath.row];
84
85       return cell;
86   }
```

The preceding code sets the first item in the myProgrammingLanguages array to the textLabel property of the first cell and so on until it reaches the number of rows in the table view (the number of the elements in the array).

By hardcoding our array, setting the items of myProgrammingLanguages inside the viewDidLoad method, and building our project, we are able to see a table view with the items of the array on each cell:

```
17   - (void)viewDidLoad {
18       [super viewDidLoad];
19
20       self.myProgrammingLanguages = @[@"Objective-C",@"Swift",@"PHP"];
21
22       // Uncomment the following line to preserve selection between presentations.
23       // self.clearsSelectionOnViewWillAppear = NO;
24
25       // Uncomment the following line to display an Edit button in the navigation bar for this
             view controller.
26       // self.navigationItem.rightBarButtonItem = self.editButtonItem;
27   }
```

Here, you can see our custom UITableViewController with three UITableViewCell classes, the items of the myProgrammingLanguages array:

Creating a cell with [tableView:dequeueReusableCellWith Identifier:@"anyReusableIdentifier" forIndexPath:indexPath] sets an identifier to the cell in order to reuse it with other content when it's no longer visible on the screen.

For example, if there is a table view with 15 elements, and in your iOS device, there are 12 cells visible in the screen, when you scroll up to see the other 3 elements, there will still be 12 cells visible. In this case, using reuse identifiers, instead of creating 15 UITableViewCells, it will create at least 13 different cells (11 fully visible cells and 2 partially visible cells), and when a cell disappears from the screen (scroll up), it is reused to load the newest visible element, appearing at the bottom.

Object immutability

Most of the classes provided by Cocoa and Cocoa Touch create objects with immutable values. In short, an immutable object has its contents set only once, and can never modify its values after that. These objects have their contents specified during their creation. The object's creation might occur in the initialization process or later, but it happens once.

Here, we can see an array that is initialized and created at the same time. Its contents are immutable:

```
/*
 ================================================
 sampleArray is allocated, initialized and
 created with the strings "Item 1" and "Item 2"
 ================================================
*/
NSArray *sampleArray = [[NSArray alloc] initWithArray:@[
            @"Item 1",
            @"Item 2"]];
//This will throw a compile time error as NSArray is not mutable.
[sampleArray addObject:@"Item 3"];
```

In the preceding line of code, `[sampleArray addObject:@"Item 3"];` will show you a compile time error as `sampleArray` is declared as an `NSArray` and not as an `NSMutableArray`, so `sampleArray` cannot have any objects added to it after it is initialized.

Now, we create another array, firstly initializing it before its creation, which might happen somewhere later in the code:

```
/*
 ================================================
 secondSampleArray is allocated and initialized
 but not yet created.
 ================================================
*/
NSArray *secondSampleArray = nil;

/*
 ================================================
 Later in our code, we can create it setting
 contents to it, but it also happens once, the
 contents won't be changed.
 ================================================
*/
secondSampleArray = @[@"Item 1", @"Item 2"];
```

You can see that we set `secondSampleArray` to `nil`, and in Objective-C, `nil` means that `secondSampleArray` has no value or an address. It is only later that we insert the two NSStrings `"Item 1"` and `"Item 2"` into `secondSampleArray` to make the size of the array 2.

Object mutability

Cocoa and Cocoa Touch also provide some mutable versions of its immutable classes. Once a mutable object is created, its contents can be partially or completely removed or modified. As we saw immutable array objects — an instance of NSArray — in the previous topic, I will now show you its mutable version, the `NSMutableArray` class, from which we will create our objects as an instance, as you can see in the following code:

```
/*
   ==============================================
   We will create now a mutable version of an
   array, using the class NSMutableArray.
   ==============================================
*/
NSMutableArray *mutableSampleArray = [[NSMutableArray alloc]
init];

/*
   ==============================================
   Now, we assign to it the list of strings:
   "String 1", "String 2", "String 3"
   ==============================================
*/
mutableSampleArray = @[@"String 1",
        @"String 2",
         @"String 3"];

/*
   ==============================================
   Later, we change the 2nd item of the list with
   the string "Replacement String", having our
   array the list:
   "String 1", "Replacement String", "String 3"
   The indexes are 0 based and starts from 0
   ==============================================
*/

[mutableSampleArray replaceObjectAtIndex:1
withObject:@"Replacement String"];
```

The mutable versions of a class (in our example, NSMutableArray) have many similarities with the original immutable version, NSArray; however, they are different classes. Intending to use methods from one that is not available for the other will generate compilation errors. Generally, immutability is what you should try to use as immutability provides a guarantee that an object won't have its value changed while you are using it. Immutability also brings performance benefits when used in things such as strings and dictionaries as mutability will bring some overhead due to the need to allocate and deallocate chunks of memory when the string or dictionary is modified.

In the case of NSArray and NSMutableArray, NSMutableArray is not thread-safe and can present weird bugs if you use multithreading. So, generally, try to use NSArray as the de facto array to use unless you really need NSMutableArray.

Inheritance

To understand inheritance, think about it as a perfect biological tree, where you have inherited some behavioral traits from your father, but more than that you have your own. Something like this happens in Objective-C when a class is inherited from another.

Basic samples are the classes whose names start with NS provided by Cocoa and Cocoa Touch, such as NSString, NSArray, and NSDictionary. They are all inherited from NSObject. Each of them has their particular methods to handle the different types of contents they hold, but everyone shares methods such as alloc and init. These two class methods, inherited from NSObject, respectively allocate memory and initialize the object:

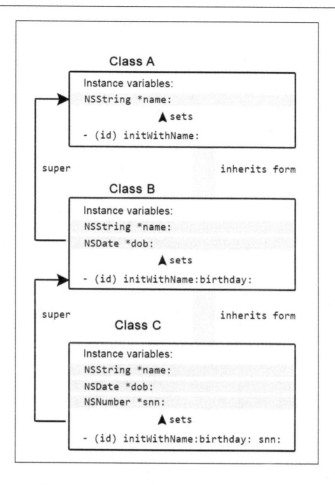

The `alloc` method will rarely be overridden, performing a single task and allocating memory to the object being created. However, another inheritance example is the `init` method, which is also inherited from `NSObject`. It received modifications in each child class, creating other initialization methods to quickly assign content to the object. These new `init` methods are inherited from the original `init` method. This is an example for `NSString`:

```
/*
===============================================
  The variable is allocated and initialized but
  still has no content, its value is nil.
=============================================== */
NSString *simpleInitializedString = [[NSString alloc] init];
/*
===============================================
  Allocated and initialized by it's custom method,
```

```
      initWithString:, inherited from init. In this
      case, the variable is initialized with a content,
      "Hey!"
============================================ */
NSString *customInitializedString = [[NSString alloc]
initWithString:@"Hey!"];
```

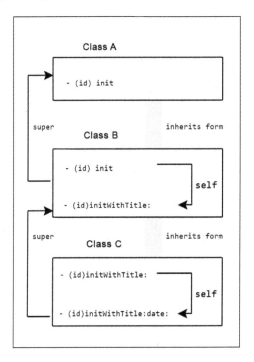

Convenience initializers

The allocation and initialization methods will allocate a chunk of memory to hold the object's content and set an empty value to it, until you assign a value yourself. The empty value differs depending on the object's type: Boolean (BOOL) objects receive the value `NO`, integers (int) receive `0`, float numbers (float) receive `0.0`, and the rest of the objects receive `nil`.

It's possible to first allocate memory for your object, and later in the code, initialize it, but it's not recommended at all.

On the other hand, you can use or even create what we call convenience initializers, which are initialization methods that receive arguments to assign different and/or additional values for instance variables.

For a better understanding, we will now create our own object class and create convenience initializers to be used in different scenarios. First, we will create a class, inherited from NSObject. It will return a float number, which is a result of a fraction of a multiplication; we will call it MultiFraction:

```
1   //
2   //  MultiFraction.h
3   //
4   //
5   //  Created by Maxim Vasilkov on 26/11/14.
6   //
7   //
8
9   #import <Foundation/Foundation.h>
10
11  @interface MultiFraction : NSObject
12
13  @end
14
```

In our header file, MultiFraction.h, we will specify the instance variables to be included in our object. It will have three values and we will use the property keyword to define the information that the MultiFraction class intends to encapsulate, which in this case are the objects of the type NSInteger, which are named firstNumerator, secondNumerator, and denominator respectively:

```
1   //
2   //  MultiFraction.h
3   //
4   //
5   //  Created by Maxim Vasilkov on 26/11/14.
6   //
7   //
8
9   #import <Foundation/Foundation.h>
10
11  @interface MultiFraction : NSObject
12
13  @property (weak, nonatomic) NSInteger *firstNumerator;
14  @property (weak, nonatomic) NSInteger *secondNumerator;
15  @property (weak, nonatomic) NSInteger *denominator;
16
17  @end
18
```

In the implementation file, `MultiFraction.m`, by omitting the `init` method, it will use the inherited initialization method from the superclass, in our case, `NSObject`, which will return a `nil` value. However, we want to implement a convenience initializer to take three arguments, save the values to be used by another method in order to perform a calculation, and return its result. Our initialization method will be named `initWithFirstNumerator:`, `secondNumerator:`, `denominator::`

```
7    //
8
9    #import "MultiFraction.h"
10
11   @implementation MultiFraction
12
13   -(id)initWithFirstNumerator:(NSNumber *)aFirstNumerator
14              secondNumerator:(NSNumber *)aSecondNumerator
15                 denominator:(NSNumber *)aDenominator {
16       |
17
18   }
19
20   @end
```

Inside our initialization method, we will store the arguments passed to our object on its respective instance variables in case we want to access any of these values in the future, instead of calculating the result directly:

```
1    //
2    //  MultiFraction.m
3    //
4    //
5    //  Created by Maxim Vasilkov on 26/11/14.
6    //
7    //
8
9    #import "MultiFraction.h"
10
11   @implementation MultiFraction
12
13   -(id) initWithFirstNumerator:(NSNumber *)aFirstNumerator
14              secondNumerator:(NSNumber *)aSecondNumerator
15                 denominator:(NSNumber *)aDenominator {
16
17       self.firstNumerator = aFirstNumerator;
18       self.secondNumerator = aSecondNumerator;
19       self.denominator = aDenominator;
20
21       return self;
22   }
23
24   @end
```

Now, we can create our object elsewhere in our Xcode project, by importing our header file:

```
#import MultiFraction.h

/*
    ================================================
```

```
   Creating a MultiFraction object with the default init method,
   inherited from NSObject.
   =============================================== */
MultiFraction *firstMultiFraction = [[MultiFraction alloc] init];
// Later, when calling a method to calculate the fraction we will
// get a nil if we handle our instance variables or an error, if
// we try to calculate as they are, nil values.


/*

   ===============================================
   Creating a MultiFraction object with the
   convenience initialization method we've created.
   =============================================== */
MultiFraction *secondMultiFraction = [[MultiFraction alloc]
        initWithFirstNumerator:25
        secondNumerator:3
        denominator:4];
// For the secondMultiFraction, when trying to calculate the
// fraction, we will get 18.75 as a float, if we take any
// argument as float when calculating the result.
```

An Objective-C programmer's responsibility

If you have experience in other programming languages, such as Java, and are coming to Objective-C now, forget about constructors, they don't exist in Objective-C. Constructors are language-level constructs that merge the allocation and initialization actions, but they have restrictions:

- They don't return anything. While the Objective-C class initialization method, + (void) initialize, does not return anything, the default—(id) init method of an Objective-C class returns an object of the type id.

- The constructor's name must be identical with the class.

- When you call the superclass, being the first statement is a must.

The last point ensures you won't deal with garbage data, but this is a restriction. In Objective-C, as in C, without this restriction, you, the programmer, have more flexibility and power, but it is also your responsibility to deal with garbage data.

The singleton pattern

Besides taking responsibility for garbage management, a good programmer should also be aware of programming design patterns. Design patterns are solutions, mostly reusable code solutions, to solve and prevent common issues. It makes a developer's life easier. In this section, I'll show you the singleton pattern. Singletons are useful if you need a single instance and need to manage that single instance such as writing to a log file. However, singletons can be misused as global variables, which makes for bad programming practice. Singletons are also implemented using static methods, which is not good for unit testing as they cannot be mocked or stubbed. So, only use a singleton in the correct context and not in every situation that you encounter.

In Objective-C, it's completely possible to have more than one instance of a class (objects) at a time. However, what if you don't need it? What if, for some reason, you need only one instance and nothing more and want to avoid multiple instances for that class? In this case, you use the singleton pattern. It ensures that there is only a single instance of a class and there is a method globally available for it.

An example already implemented by Apple in the `UIScreen` class is the `mainScreen` method. It's globally available and returns a instance of its class, ensuring it's the only one. The reason is obvious, we don't need more than one main screen. It's called from anywhere in your project, as shown here:

```
[UIScreen mainScreen]
```

When you first call the method, the instance is not created yet. It will then be initialized and returned as expected; however, from the second time the method is called, it doesn't create a new instance but returns the existing one. That's how it ensures only one instance exists. Let's go through the following sample code:

In the header file, we will first create a global method to access its instance:

```
@interface connectionLibrary : NSObject
+ (connectionLibrary*)mySharedInstance;
@end
```

Then, in your implementation file, implement the method, as shown here:

```
+ (connectionLibrary*)mySharedInstance {
  // First, we create a static variable to hold our instance
  static connectionLibrary *_mySharedInstance = nil;
  /*
    Create a static variable to ensure the instance will be
initialized only once
  */
  static dispatch_once_t initOnce;
```

```
/*
    Now, the core of the singleton pattern is GCD, Grand
    Central Dispatch, that executes a block where the
    initialization method is never called once the class
    was already initiated.
*/

    dispatch_once(&initOnce, ^{
    _mySharedInstance = [[connectionLibrary alloc] init];
});
  return _mySharedInstance;
}
```

Now, you can initialize and access this instance from anywhere in your code:

```
connectionLibrary *sharedInstance = [connectionLibrary
mySharedInstance];
```

Creating @property

There are two ways to store data in objects, they are properties and instance variables. The latter should be used just for objects and values exclusively handled by the class itself, not from outside. Properties, on the other hand, for objects and values are accessible from outside (by other classes).

While using instance variables, you can create public or private ones. The difference is basically where you declare them as sometimes you need them to be accessible by other classes, while in other situations, there is no need to expose them to other classes. If they are declared in the header file as part of the @interface block, they have public scope and if declared in the implementation file as part of the @ implementation block, they have private scope. Generally, they should be private:

```
@implementation Book {
   int _numberOfPages;
   int _numberOfChapters;
   NSArray *_authorsInfo;
}
```

To easily understand your code, instance variable starts with an underscore; it doesn't affect the way they work, but it's a convention highly recommended to be followed.

Instance variables are private and accessible only by the class or subclass, plus it is encapsulated by the class, which contains it, while a property is public and can be accessed by other classes. Properties can also be private when declared as part of the class extension, but they are often public since you want to access them from the outside. By accessing, there are two options, get or set their content. Objective-C automatically generates getters and setters for each declared property. In order to declare a property with public scope, do it in your header file as shown here:

```
@interface Book : NSObject
@property (strong, nonatomic) NSString *chapterNote;
@end
```

The preceding code mostly tells other classes that the Book class has a public property, which can be accessed by chapterNote:

```
Book *objCBook = [[Book alloc] init];
// This is our setter, we are setting an value to it
objCBook.chapterNote = "I really love this chapter";
//This non dot syntax setter is also valid
[objCBook setChapterNote:@"I really love this chapter"];
/*
   This is our getter, we get the value hold on chapterNote
   and save it in myLastNote
*/
NSString *myLastNote = objCBook.chapterNote
```

Creating custom methods

In Objective-C, methods when declared start with – or +, as you will see in this section. The latter declares a static method, while the former, – , declares instance methods. As a developer, you won't declare static methods (starting with +) regularly.

Static methods are generally used if you don't need an instance of a class in that method, while instance methods are used when you need that instance to modify its state. Instance methods are more commonly used as instance methods give you access to a class instance variables.

To declare a method, you follow a syntax. You will need the following entities:

- The symbol to specify the type of the method
- The type of the data it will return
- The method's name

- For each parameter:
  - ○ The type of parameter
  - ○ The name of parameter
- Your code inside the method

Following our example, in `mySpecialTableViewController`, let's declare an instance method that will take one parameter, a string (`NSString`). Our method will return the content of the `myProgrammingLanguages` array as a single string. Each object will be followed by the parameter given. Our method will be called `convertToStringWith`.

Before we go to the implementation file, the method must be declared in the header file, not doing this may cause errors when calling the method because the header file defines what methods are exposed to the outside.

```
1   //
2   //   mySpecialTableViewController.h
3   //   BookSample
4   //
5   //   Created by Maxim Vasilkov on 27/11/14.
6   //   Copyright (c) 2014 Arthur Alves. All rights reserved.
7   //
8
9   #import <UIKit/UIKit.h>
10
11  @interface mySpecialTableViewController : UITableViewController
12
13  @property (strong, nonatomic) NSArray *myProgrammingLanguages;
14
15  // If you don't declare your method here you may get errors when calling it.
16  -(NSString *)convertToStringWith:(NSString *)placeBetween;
17
18  @end
```

Now, move to the implementation file and implement the method:

```
40
41  -(NSString *)convertToStringWith:(NSString *)placeBetween
42  {
43      return [self.myProgrammingLanguages componentsJoinedByString:placeBetween];
44  };
```

In this case, when calling the method, if the `myProgrammingLanguages` array contains the string values: `"Objective-C"`, `"Swift"`, and `"PHP"`, the result would be a unique string with the passed parameter between the values, as shown in the following examples:

```
20    self.myProgrammingLanguages = @[@"Objective-C",@"Swift",@"PHP"];
21
22    /*
23     This string will contain the value: "Objective-C/Swift/PHP"
24    */
25    NSString *firstString = [self convertToStringWith:@"/"];
26
27    /*
28     This string will contain the value: "Objective-C SPACE Swift SPACE PHP"
29    */
30    NSString *secondString = [self convertToStringWith:@" SPACE "];
```

There are occasions when you don't want to pass any parameter to a method. It's possible; you just need the type of the data returned and the name of the method:

```
-(BOOL) doYouLikeThisBook
{
    return true;
}
```

There are two special cases about the type of the data retuned by a method, when you don't know it and when you won't return anything. In the first case, you should use id, as shown here:

```
-(id) initSomethingWithoutKnowingTheType
{
    self = [super class];
    return self;
}
```

On the other hand, if you don't want to return nothing, use void.

```
-(void) storeUserDetails:(NSString *)userName withID(int)userID
{
    self.name = userName;
    self.id = userID;
}
```

String formatting

When dealing with different types of objects, especially inserting/appending them into a string, you need to specify their types inside the string, for which we use format specifiers. Printing to the console, for example, requires a string to be printed; it's the only accepted format. Let's see how to insert different objects inside it, to be properly printed to the console:

```
// Here we print a message, it's already a string.
NSLog(@"I'm a message. A string");
```

However, if you want to print a value stored in a property or instance variable, you should specify its type inside in order to properly replace it with the value outside:

```
/*
    Now we print the string value stored on a property
    The console will print the message:
    "Hello, Mr. Gaius Julius Caesar"
*/
NSString *myStringObject = @"Gaius Julius Caesar";
NSLog(@"Hello, Mr. %@", myStringObject);
```

Notice %@ inside the message. It specifies that the value is a string. This is how we can specify the object's type, using a percentage sign, %, followed by a specific keyword (conversion specifier). Using a different conversion specifier for a string will result in compilation error.

Mostly, specifiers support more than one data type:

The format specifier	Supported object's type
%d	Integer (signed int), 32-bit
%u	Integer (unsigned int), 32-bit
%x	Integer (unsigned int) as hexadecimal value, 32-bit
%o	Integer (unsigned int) as octal value, 32-bit
%%	print "%"
%f	Float, double (point float number), 64-bit
%e	Float, double (point float number) in scientific notation, 64-bit
%g	Float, double (point float number) as %e if the exponent is less than –4, otherwise as %f, 64 bit
%c	Unsigned character (unsigned char), 8 bit
%S	An array of 16-bit Unicode characters, which terminates with a null pointer

The format specifier	Supported object's type
%p	A void pointer character (void *) in hexadecimal, starting with 0x
%a	Double (point float number) in scientific notation, starting with 0x and one hexadecimal digit before the decimal point using a lowercase p to introduce the exponent, 64 bit
%F	Double (point float number) in decimal notation
%hhd	BOOL

Summary

In this chapter, we were able to see objects in detail, how inheritance works and how you can use it to create even more powerful classes. You learned about an object's mutability and immutability, how instance variables and property work, what they are, and how to create them besides allocation, initialization, and custom methods, and how to create your own. In the next chapter, we will cover application data management such as resource optimization, caching, and data saving. So, see you in the next chapter.

5
Managing Your Application Data

In this chapter, you will be introduced to the concept of managing your application data to ensure that your application will perform at an optimal level during runtime. The following topics will be covered:

- Resource optimization
- Disk and memory caching
- Serialization
- Different forms of data saving
- Pros and cons of various data saving methods

We will also cover some common pitfalls and assumptions that people commonly associate with the development of iOS applications. One example will be image loading, where if the developers are not careful in planning the proper architecture of their application, they will encounter situations where the application will lag or run out of memory and lead to an application crash.

Device memory

As with all computing devices, iPads and iPhones have a finite amount of memory and you may be tempted to develop applications without any concern about the memory usage. Doing so is not ideal for development as memory optimizing and management should always be at the top of your mind when doing any type of development, regardless of whatever platform you will be developing on.

Let's take a look at the amount of memory that each of the iOS devices have, and we will start with iPhones:

	iPhone 4S	iPhone 5	iPhone 5C	iPhone 5S
RAM	512 MB	1 GB	1 GB	1 GB

Here is the RAM for iPads:

	iPad Air	iPad Mini 2	iPad Mini Wi-Fi + Cellular	iPad 2 Wi-Fi + 3G	iPad Mini Wi-Fi	iPad 3 Wi-Fi	iPad 3 Wi-Fi + Cellular	iPad 4 Wi-Fi	iPad 2 Wi-Fi
RAM	1 GB	1 GB	512 MB	512 MB	512 MB	1 GB	1 GB	1 GB	512 MB

Now, the amount of memory does look impressive as you fondly remember the days of old, where your old desktop ran on 256 MB of RAM, but do remember that iOS does not let you play with the full 512 MB or 1 GB RAM. The OS will allocate some to system processes in your device, and you will only get a subset of the available RAM for your application.

In your application, everything will occupy memory and storage space. Some of the biggest culprits are binary assets, such as videos and images, which can be total resource hogs to even your class objects that can take up precious space if you do not take note of them when doing your development. So, let's start with image optimization as almost every application will make use of images in one way or another.

Image optimization

Any application will look boring and drab without the usage of .png and some nice images. However, one thing about images is that they take up much more memory than their file size implies. A single 1 MB .png file can occupy double or triple their memory size when loaded into the memory. The reason is because PNG is basically a compressed file format, such as a ZIP file. So, all the image data is compressed into a PNG file and when your application needs to display your PNG image. It needs to load the PNG file into memory, uncompress it, and then it will be able to get the image data to be used by your code and will consume more memory in the process. So, if your application has 20 MB of PNG files, you are easily looking at 40 MB or more of RAM allocation just for images. So, a few tips for image optimization are:

- Save your image as PNG-8 instead of PNG-24 as PNG-8 consumes less RAM than their equivalent PNG-24. Only use PNG-24 if you need the alpha channel for transparency. The difference between PNG-8 and PNG-24 is the image quality and the number of colors that you can have. The 8 and 24 means 8-bits per pixel and 24-bits per pixel respectively. So, PNG-8 can only support up to 256 colors while PNG-24 can support up to 16 million colors, so PNG-24 is the best option if you need to display images with a lot of colors such as photographs, while logos and user interface elements such as icons can probably get by with PNG-8. PNG-24 also supports alpha transparency, which is good for images that need to have a transparent background. So, knowing which format to use in which situation will help you in reducing the memory consumption of your application.

- If you can use JPG files, then use them as they are a lossy format, and it means that you will get a bit of image degradation, but generally the image degradation is almost invisible to the naked eye. However, note that JPG files do not support alpha transparency.

PNG is a lossless format, which means that there is no image degradation when you use PNG files, but it comes at a price that it consumes more RAM when loaded into your device compared to a JPG, which is a lossy format.

So, keep PNG files and JPG files to an absolute minimum if you can and only use them if you have to.

Lazy loading

What is lazy loading? It is a design pattern or a way of doing things in software design where you load a resource such as a PNG, MP3 file, and so on only at the time when it is needed. This helps to mitigate the problem of insufficient memory instead of loading all your resources at once. You only load it when you need it in a "lazy" manner. There is also one more advantage, that is, it minimizes the start up time of your application since you only load the resources on demand and this takes less time to load. So, you gain a speed boost in terms of time.

Imagine you have multiple UIViews where each view has 10 UIImages, but only one view can be seen at any one time. Without proper thought, you will be tempted to write code to load all 10 UIImages for all the UIViews at once. However, upon further reflection, the question arises as to whether there is a need to do so. It would be better if you refactor your code to load the 10 UIImages only when that UIView is visible to the user and then clean it up once the user is not viewing it and load the next batch of UIImages from the next UIView, which will be visible to the user. This will add a bit more of coding for you, but the trade-off in terms of efficient memory usage will be worth it.

This is one of the simplest implementations where we just override the getter method of a class:

```
- (A_Class *)aObject {
    if (aObject == nil) {//Check if the object exists and if not
        aObject = [[A_Class alloc] init];//then create the object
    }

    return aObject;//returns the object
}
```

You can put the preceding code in place of the normal getter method of your class. The preceding code checks whether the object does or does not exists, and if it does not exist, then it will create the object. However, if the object already exists, then it will not create it again.

Control creation

Controls are part and parcel of every iOS application and they also consume memory on your device and every instance will consume bytes and bits of memory. When you are creating a lot of UITableViewCell class, for example, you will be looking at a control that is consuming a lot of memory sooner or later.

Also, tasks such as loading images and getting data from a remote server are considered as slow processes and will slow down your application. I am sure that you have used iOS apps where when you scroll down a UITableView view object you will see a noticeable lag as new images are loaded into the newly revealed cells. In this world, where people are used to images loading quickly on their desktop and mobile phones, such slowness and laggy UI are not acceptable and can mean the difference between a user staying engaged with your application or uninstalling your application.

The fundamental mantra is that you must not let your users wait for 1 second or even 1 millisecond more than what is absolutely necessary. One tip to compensate for the perceived slowness of an application is to have a simple animation such as fading in an image after showing a spinner in order to give the user the perception that the application is not actually very slow since there is an animation playing.

Reusing your controls is a must if you are experiencing huge memory usage, which is impacting the usability of your iOS application. Later on, we will cover how to use the tool called **Instrument** in Xcode to monitor the memory usage. Creating objects is an expensive process and has a performance cost.

If you need to create an object on the fly over a short period of time, such as scrolling quickly through a UITableView view object, you will experience some lag as your code will be creating new UITableViewCell class instead of reusing old ones.

Reusing UITableViewCell is a lot faster and will enhance the performance of your application. Luckily, Apple has already created code for us to reuse a cell, which can be implemented easily with a few lines of code. So, let's look at the dequeueReusableCellWithIdentifier method as a good example with the following code:

```
- (UITableViewCell *)tableView:(UITableView *)tableView
cellForRowAtIndexPath:(NSIndexPath *)indexPath {
    UITableViewCell *cell = [tableView
dequeueReusableCellWithIdentifier:@"Cell"];
    if (!cell) {
        //create a new cell
    }

    //Do what we need with our cell here

    return cell;
}
```

Looking at the preceding code, you can see that we attempt to assign a cell using the dequeueReusableCellWithIdentifier method, then it will return a pointer to that cell if it already exists. Next, our code (!cell) will check whether that pointer is not nil, then it will create the cell. This is the exact same technique we used in the previous section *Lazy loading*, except that we apply this technique to an iOS control, which in this case, is a UITableViewCell object. These few lines of code serve three functions:

- This helps to prevent a situation where your app is lagging when you are scrolling up as it eliminates the need to create new instances of UITableViewCell.

- If you have 1,000 rows of data and only 4 rows are visible on screen at any given time, then it makes no sense to create 1,000 UITableViewCell when you only need to create five. A few other cells can be partially visible and hence need to be created too. So, the five cells will only be created as it needs to be visible to the user while the remaining cells are not loaded.

- While a single UITableViewCell class occupies a lot of memory, storing 1,000 of them is not easy, and through a few extra lines of code, you can avoid unnecessary memory usage and use the memory you save for other parts of your code.

Caching

Caching is a concept where you store resources on disk or memory for faster access. Caching will occupy more space, but in situations where you need to worry more about loading speed than memory, caching can be a very good technique to use. Consider this common scenario:

- Downloading a large file such as an image or even a movie
- Write the file to a disk
- Read the files from the disk and display them

If you follow the normal method as mentioned earlier, a bottleneck that you will face is slow loading of the file from disk. Disk access can be as slow as 10,000 or even 1,000,000 slower than memory access and it won't make a good user experience as the user will be kept waiting while your app is loading the files from disk. Caching will help slow this problem as your file is saved to memory where read access is faster.

This is good from a user point of view as they do not need to wait a long time for the file to be loaded and can help to optimize the user experience of your application since every second wasted can lead to the user moving away from your application. Caching on disk or memory has its pros and cons as illustrated in the following table:

	Disk	Memory
Storage	Persistent, as data is not lost when device is switched off	Ephemeral, as data is lost when device is switched off
Speed	Slow	Fast
Storage size	Large	Small, as memory is generally lesser than disk storage

So as a rule of thumb, it will be best to do all caching on memory first and then move to caching on disk only when your application is running low on memory or you experience memory warning errors. If you are downloading large files such as movies, you will need to store the movie file on disk since the file normally will not be able to fit into memory.

As a sidenote, caching uses a few algorithms for implementation, such as **Most Recently Used (MRU)** or **Least Recently Used (LRU)**. MRU means the cache will discard the most recently used items first when the cache is full, while LRU is the reverse opposite where the least recently used items will be discarded instead. The implementation strategy is out of the scope of this book and it is up to the manufacturer to decide.

Fortunately, we do not need to write a lot of code to implement efficient caching. There are a few iOS caching libraries that we can use and they are available for us to use. So, in this section, we will look at one of the most popular caching libraries.

SDWebImage

The first library we will be looking at is called SDWebImage. The source code can be downloaded via a Git clone from `https://github.com/rs/SDWebImage`, and it comes with a demo project too. So, let's look at the important parts of this demo project. I have summarized the steps for you:

1. Open the Xcode project.
2. Open up `masterviewcontroller`.
3. Import `UIImageView+WebCache.h`.
4. Look for the `cellforrowatindexpath` method.
5. Call this method `setImageWithURL:placeholderImage`.

Now, let's look into each of these steps in detail:

Open the `SDWebImage Demo.xcodeproj` project and run it. You should see the following screen, which is a list of table view cells with images and text:

If you tap on a table view cell, it will show this screen, which shows the larger size of the image that you tapped on:

Next, open up `MasterViewController` and look for the following piece of code:

```
- (UITableViewCell *)tableView:(UITableView *)tableView
cellForRowAtIndexPath:(NSIndexPath *)indexPath
{
    static NSString *CellIdentifier = @"Cell";

    UITableViewCell *cell = [tableView
    dequeueReusableCellWithIdentifier:CellIdentifier];
    if (cell == nil)
    {
        cell = [[UITableViewCell alloc]
        initWithStyle:UITableViewCellStyleDefault
        reuseIdentifier:CellIdentifier];
    }

    cell.textLabel.text = [NSString stringWithFormat:@"Image
#%d", indexPath.row];
    cell.imageView.contentMode =
    UIViewContentModeScaleAspectFill;
    [cell.imageView setImageWithURL:[NSURL
    URLWithString:[_objects objectAtIndex:indexPath.row]]
```

```
            placeholderImage:[UIImage
            imageNamed:@"placeholder"]
             options:indexPath.row == 0 ?
            SDWebImageRefreshCached : 0];

        return cell;
}
```

This is where the code will get the image from the server and then cache it on the device.

To implement this in your own code, you need to import `UIImageView+WebCache.h` and then call the `setImageWithURL:placeholderImage:` method, where you can add in your own placeholder PNG and JPG image to replace `@"placeholder"`.

So, when you run the app again you will notice that images are not pulled from server again, but are instead served from the cache on the device, so you will see that the images load faster as a result.

Object serialization

What is serialization? This is a question that a lot of people find hard to explain or understand. Serialization is the method or concept where we convert data structures or objects into a format for it to be stored in memory or disk for storage, or to be transmitted across a network link. It can also assist in memory management as it provides an alternative mechanism where we save some files to disk instead of memory, which is usually the case for big files, such as movie files. Serialization formats include JSON, XML, YAML, and so on. And luckily for iOS developers, Apple provides us with a robust framework that helps us take away the low-level code when we want to do serialization. So, when we want to store our data structures or objects in memory or disk, we can use Apple's frameworks such as Core Data or NSCoding, which provides an abstraction layer and hides away the lower-level coding for us.

When it comes to data saving or serialization, we tend to stick with the one method that we are most familiar with. However, this is not a good way of doing things as various methods have their pros and cons, and we should consider our use case before we decide on the best method. To this extent, Apple has provided us with a few different methods for data serialization and it is up to us, the developers, to decide which method suits us best. One of the simplest ways is to use NSCoding. What is NSCoding? NSCoding is basically a protocol provided by Apple for you to encode and decode your data into a buffer, which can then be persisted to disk for persistent storage.

Usage of the NSCoding protocol also involves the NSKeyedArchiver and NSKeyedUnarchiver methods as NSCoding is a protocol with delegate methods for serializing our data structure and custom object into a format that can be stored in memory or disk. NSKeyedArchiver and NSKeyedUnarchiver are the methods that will actually do the work of storing our serialized data into disk for persistent storage. So to kick things off, we will use an example to help us understand how serializing and archiving works for iOS applications.

Use the listed steps for the following example:

1. Add the NSCoding protocol to your custom object.

2. Implement encodeWithCoder and initWithCoder and assign the values you wish to store.

3. Call the archiveRootObject and unarchiveObjectWithFile methods to save your serialized data to disk and load it from the disk respectively.

4. For example, we create a custom object called OurCustomObject, and then to use the NSCoding protocol, we need to add it to our interface declaration:

```
@interface OurCustomObject : NSObject <NSCoding>
{
    bool isReset;
    NSString *userName;
    int score;
}
@property (nonatomic, retain) NSString *userName;
@property (nonatomic, assign) bool  isReset;
@property (nonatomic, assign) int score;
@end
```

5. Then, we need to write the encodeWithCoder method to save the data:

```
- (void)encodeWithCoder:(NSCoder *)coder {
    //do encoding to save the data
    [coder encodeBool:isReset forKey:@"isReset"];
    [coder encodeObject:userName    forKey:@"userName"];
    [coder encodeInt:score forKey:@"score"];
}
```

To load the data back into our objects, we add in the initWithCoder method:

```
- (id)initWithCoder:(NSCoder *)decoder {
    if (self = [super init]) {
        self.isReset = [decoder
        decodeBoolForKey:@"isReset"];
        self.userName = [decoder
        decodeObjectForKey:@"userName"];
```

```
    self.score = [decoder decodeIntForKey:@"score"];
}
return self;
}
```

6. Now that we have the code to encode and decode the data into a serialized format, we need to put in the actual code to save it to disk on our device, so we can use `NSKeyedArchiver` to do the actual writing to disk, while we use `NSKeyedUnarchiver` to get the data from the disk:

```
OurCustomObject *ourObj = [[OurCustomObject alloc] init];
    ourObj.userName = @"John Doe";
    ourObj.isReset   = true;
    ourObj.score = 99;
//get our file path
NSArray *paths =
NSSearchPathForDirectoriesInDomains(NSDocumentDirectory,
NSUserDomainMask, YES);
    NSString *documentsDirectoryPath = [paths
    objectAtIndex:0];
    NSString *filePath = [documentsDirectoryPath
    stringByAppendingPathComponent:@"OurData"];
    [NSKeyedArchiver archiveRootObject: ourObj
    toFile:filePath];
```

7. Then to load our object from disk, we just use the following code:

```
OurCustomObject *ourObj2 = [NSKeyedUnarchiver
unarchiveObjectWithFile:filePath];
NSLog(@"Score is %d", [ourObj2 score]);
NSLog(@"Name is %@", [ourObj2 userName]);
```

There is no need to call `initWithCoder` and `encodeWithCoder` anywhere in our code as those method calls are called when you call `unarchiveObjectWithFile` and `archiveRootObject`. However, you need to implement `initWithCoder` and `encodeWithCoder` as these two methods need to contain the necessary code to encode and decode the `isReset`, `userName`, and `score` variables that form `OurCustomObject`. As you can see, `NSCoding` is a relatively powerful way to store data to disk compared to `NSUserDefaults`, and the code is quite easy to understand and write. However, if you need more power features for data storage, `NSCoding` will not be the best choice and Core Data will be the better option as it has more features such as being able to perform queries, being optimized for speed, support for different serialization formats such as XML, SQLite, or NSDate, among other benefits.

SQLite

SQLite, for those familiar with **Relational DataBase Management System (RDBMS)**, is a database based on the relational model. A SQLiteis, a RDBMS that is available for us in iOS, has a lot of the features and functions of RDBMS that many people are familiar with, such as ACID properties, queries, and so on. Core Data is Apple's framework for data storage and you can use Core Data to store data into a SQLite database. However, there are some cases when you need to use SQLite instead of Core Data. So, I will elaborate further on this:

- SQLite as a database is available on multiple platforms besides iOS. So this means that if you are developing an application that runs on multiple platforms or has the possibility to run on other non-iOS platforms, SQLite will be the option for you to seriously consider since you will avoid framework lock-in using Core Data. SQLite also is faster than NSCoding, plus it adds querying functionality, which is not possible if you use `NSUserDefaults`.

- Also, if you have experience with SQLite and your use case for data storage is very straightforward along with no experience with Core Data, then you should choose SQLite.

- It does not require a **Model-View-Controller (MVC)** conceptual model.

Now, this does not mean that SQLite should be the default data storage solution for you when you need to store data to disk. This is because there are other options such as Core Data and various other factors such as speed and ease of coding, which will play a big part in your decision-making as we will see later in this chapter and the chapter on Core Data later on.

SQLite versus Core Data

Core Data is a rich and sophisticated object graph management framework with a lot of bells and whistles that you require for complex use cases. In the *Introduction to Core Data Programming Guide*, Apple mentions that the Core Data framework provides generalized and automated solutions to common tasks associated with object life cycle and object graph management, including persistence, which means it prevents you from writing a lot of code to do your everyday data storage tasks.

Core Data uses models that are your objects and these are the model in the commonly used MVC architecture. These enable you to store whole objects and it ties in very closely with the controller and view classes of your iOS application. So, developers who are using MVC architectures will have no problem absorbing the Core Data concepts and models.

The tools for development using the Core Data framework is tied in deeply into Xcode and it enables developers to quickly write code and lay out their data models in a fast and efficient manner, and thus, save you time, which allows you to spend it on other parts of the project.

Core Data framework is also available for the Mac OS, and this enables reusability of your code if you intend to create a Mac version of your application.

With Apple's iCloud storage and computing platform, you can use Core Data to take advantage of iCloud to sync your application and user data across multiple devices such as iPads and so on. iOS 8 has tighter integration with iCloud with the introduction of the CloudKit framework, which has new functionality such as allowing partial download of datasets and all this is only possible using Core Data.

SQLite is a pure RDBMS and many people confuse Core Data with SQLite. SQLite is a RDBMS, pure and simple. So, it has a lot of the features that you will associate with RDBMSes, such as ACID properties, queries, and so on. However, that is where it ends. Core Data is an abstraction layer on top of a data store, which can be SQLite or other forms of data persistence, such as XML files. So, using Core Data will still enable you to store data in SQLite, but there will be some occasions when you prefer to use SQLite over Core Data.

If data portability is an important feature for you, then using SQLite should be your preferred choice as SQLite is platform-independent, while Core Data is for Apple platforms only. So, if you use SQLite, you can be assured that your data files can be moved and accessed on almost any platform that supports SQLite, not only Apple-supported platforms.

Core Data ultimately is an abstraction layer between your code and the database. However, sometimes you want to get down to the lower levels of your code and avoid abstraction layers to understand how the code works. So, using SQLite will allow you to do that, as it allows you to do low level optimization if you are working with large datasets. Core Data can also be used to abstract the Sqlite access to save on development time and make your code cleaner.

Ultimately, there are no hard and fast rules on when and where to use Core Data or SQLite. On every engineering project, there are questions and decisions to be made, which encompass factors such as amount of resources and platform scalability since Core Data only supports Apple platforms and if you intend to support non-Apple platforms. Core Data might not be a good choice. So, using the Core Data framework allows you to have a rapid solution for simple applications, but it also ties you into Apple's framework, which impedes data portability as if you create an application where a user's data such as game data needs to be present on another non-Apple device. You will encounter a technical lock-in if you use Core Data.

On the other hand, SQLite allows ease of tweaking and optimization for various reasons. In the end, the complexity of your use case, data model, and requirements of your platform will be the factors that will help you make a good decision on the right option to choose.

Summary

In summary, this chapter covered the management of your application data with regards to caching data to memory and data storage on to disk. We also covered the pros and cons of using the various storage frameworks for various situations and did a few code examples on using the NSCoding protocol and the SDWebImage open source caching framework.

This chapter covers a bit of Core Data, which will help us in the next chapter as we deep dive into Core Data along with some code examples. The next chapter will be all about Core Data and its uses.

6
Using Core Data for Persistence

If you do any serious form of iOS development, data persistence is something that you are bound to come across sooner rather than later. After all, what good is an app when it does not save your user data and requires you to fill it in again when you start the app again subsequently?

This is where data persistence comes into the scene. As it is, iOS developers have a few options for data persistence ranging from property list, binary format to SQLite, and so on.

As with these options, each has its good and bad points, and when to use each particular method of persistence will depend on your use case. You will also have to write specific code to handle data persistence for SQLite and binary data. Core Data can be used to store data in **plist**, SQLite, and other formats, which makes it a pretty powerful framework in itself as we will see in this chapter.

In this chapter, we will cover the following topics:

- Why use Core Data?
- Core Data concepts
- Putting Core Data into practice
- Getting into the code
- Saving data into the persistent store
- Deleting data from the persistent store

Why use Core Data?

You might be thinking to yourself, "Why do I have to learn another method when there are so many ways already available to us?" So, in this section and on the following pages, we will see why Core Data is the preferred way to store data on iOS and the Mac OS platform.

The first thing you need to know is that Core Data is not another method of data persistence per se; it is actually an abstraction over SQLite, plists, and so on. This means that you can actually use Apple's Core Data API to save your data into the persistent store just by using the Core Data API without needing to write plist-specific or SQLite-specific code if you choose to store your data as plists or SQLite respectively. This abstraction layer illustrates the basic concept of why Core Data is so powerful.

Now that you have your mind blown, the abstraction layer means that you can just use the Core Data APIs, and the abstraction layer will handle all the storage-specific code for you as all this high-level stuff will help you get away from writing low-level stuff, specific for each different data persistent format such as SQLite, property list, and so on.

Core Data integrates very tightly with iCloud and provides a host of benefits related to iCloud, such as data synching. It also allows you to do entity modeling with the benefits of querying while making it very fast in terms of access speed plus giving you the freedom to choose the storage type that can be SQLite, XML, or NSDate. With all the benefits that Core Data provides, it comes with a trade-off in which you need to write a bit more code compared to NSCoding. However, as we will see later, the amount of code is not a lot, and the Core Data framework is not complex to understand too.

A few more things that I would like to mention about Core Data is that since it is so tightly integrated into the Apple platforms, you can have access to a lot of related classes such as `NSFetchedResultsController` that make it easy for you to get your entities into `UITableViews`. It also has a nice graphical object model editor that allows you to easily think about your object/entity design and conceptualize it easily using Core Data's visual tools. With all these benefits, let's dig into Core Data now.

Understanding Core Data concepts

Core Data allows you to store your data in a variety of storage types. So, if you want to use other types of memory store, such as XML or binary store, you can use the following store types:

- `NSSQLiteStoreType`: This is the option you most commonly use as it just stores your database in a SQLite database.

- `NSXMLStoreType`: This will store your data in an XML file, which is slower, but you can open the XML file and it will be human readable. This has the option of helping you debug errors relating to storage of data. However, do note that this storage type is only available for Mac OS X.

- `NSBinaryStoreType`: This occupies the least amount of space and also produces the fastest speed as it stores all data as a binary file, but the entire database binary need to be able to fit into memory in order to work properly.

- `NSInMemoryStoreType`: This stores all data in memory and provides the fastest access speed. However, the size of your database to be saved cannot exceed the available free space in memory since the data is stored in memory. However, do note that memory storage is ephemeral and is not stored permanently to disk.

Next, there are two concepts that you need to know, and they are:

- Entity
- Attributes

Now, these terms may be foreign to you. However, for those of you who have knowledge of databases, you will know it as tables and columns. So, to put it in an easy-to-understand picture, think of Core Data entities as your database tables and Core Data attributes as your database columns.

So, Core Data handles data persistence using the concepts of entity and attributes, which are abstract data types, and actually saves the data into plists, SQLite databases, or even XML files (applicable only to the Mac OS). Going back a bit in time, Core Data is a descendant of Apple's **Enterprise Objects Framework (EOF)**, which was introduced by NeXT, Inc in 1994, and EOF is an **Object-relational mapper (ORM)**, but Core Data itself is not an ORM. Core Data is a framework for managing the object graph, and one of its powerful capabilities is that it allows you to work with extremely large datasets and object instances that normally would not fit into memory by putting objects in and out of memory when necessary. Core Data will map the Objective-C data type to the related data types, such as string, date, and integer, which will be represented by `NSString`, `NSDate`, and `NSNumber` respectively. So, as you can see, Core Data is not a radically new concept that you need to learn as it is grounded in the simple database concepts that we all know. Since entity and attributes are abstract data types, you cannot access them directly as they do not exist in physical terms. So to access them, you need to use the Core Data classes and methods provided by Apple.

The number of classes for Core Data is actually pretty long, and you won't be using all of them regularly. So, here is a list of the more commonly used classes:

Class name	Example use case
NSManagedObject	Accessing attributes and rows of data
NSManagedObjectContext	Fetching data and saving data
NSManagedObjectModel	Storage
NSFetchRequest	Requesting data
NSPersistentStoreCoordinator	Persisting data
NSPredicate	Data query

Now, explore each of these classes in depth:

- NSManagedObject: This is a record that you will use and perform operations on and all entities will extend this class.

- NSManagedObjectContext: This can be thought of as an intelligent scratchpad where temporary copies are brought into it after you fetch objects from the persistent store. So, any modifications done in this intelligent scratchpad are not saved until you save those changes into the persistent store, NSManagedObjectModel. Think of this as a collection of entities or a database schema, if you will.

- NSFetchRequest: This is an operation that describes the search criteria, which you will use to retrieve data from the persistent store, a kind of the common SQL query that most developers are familiar with.

- NSPersistentStoreCoordinator: This is like the glue that associates your managed object context and persistent.

- NSPersistentStoreCoordinator: Without this, your modifications will not be saved to the persistent store.

- NSPredicate: This is used to define logical conditions used in a search or for filtering in-memory. Basically, it means that NSPredicate is used to specify how data is to be fetched or filtered and you can use it together with NSFetchRequest as NSFetchRequest has a predicate property.

Putting it into practice

Now that we have covered the basics of Core Data, let's proceed with some code examples of how to use Core Data, where we use Core Data to store customer details in a Customer table. The information we want to store is:

- name
- email
- phone_number
- address
- age

> Do note that all attribute names must be in lowercase and should not have spaces in them. For example, we will use Core Data to store customer details mentioned earlier as well as retrieve, update, and delete the customer records using the Core Data framework and methods.

1. First, we will select **File** | **New** | **File** and then select **iOS** | **Core Data**:

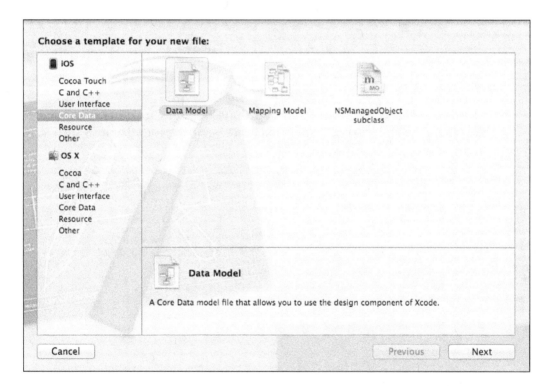

2. Then, we will proceed to create a new **Entity** called **Customer** by clicking on the **Add Entity** button in the bottom left of the screen, as shown here:

3. Then, we will proceed to add in the attributes for our **Customer** entity and give them the appropriate **Type**, which can be **String** for attributes such as **name** or **address** and **Integer 16** for **age**:

4. Lastly, we need to add **CoreData.framework**, as shown in the following screenshot:

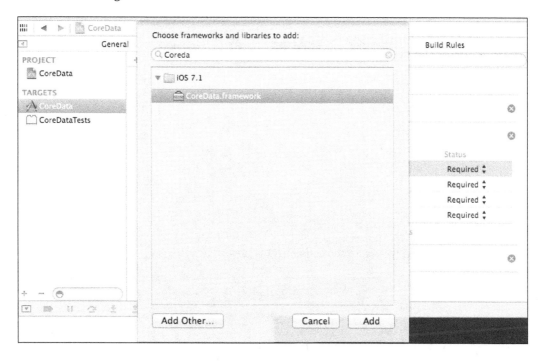

5. So with this, we have created a Core Data model class consisting of a Customer entity and some attributes. Do note that all core model classes have the .xcdatamodeld file extension and for us, we can save our Core Data model as Model.xcdatamodeld.

6. Next, we will create a sample application that uses Core Data in the following ways:

   ° Saving a record

   ° Searching for a record

   ° Deleting a record

   ° Loading records

Now, I won't cover the usage of UIKit and storyboard, but instead focus on the core code needed to give you an example of Core Data works. So, to start things off, here are a few screenshots of the application for you to have a look at to see what we'll do:

- This is the main screen when you start the app:

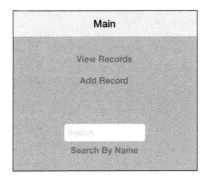

- The screen to insert a record is shown here:

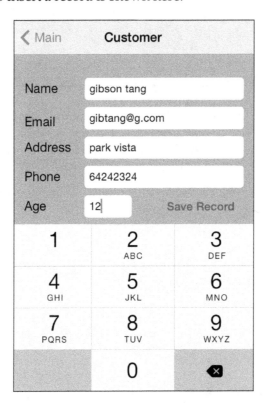

- The screen to list all records from our persistent store is as follows:

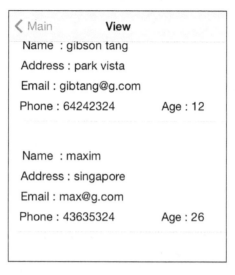

- By deleting a record from the persistent store, you will get the following output:

Getting into the code

Let's get started with our code examples:

1. For our code, we will first declare some Core Data objects in our
    `AppDelegate` class inside our `AppDelegate.h` file such as:

    ```
    @property (readonly, strong, nonatomic)
    NSManagedObjectContext
    *managedObjectContext;
    @property (readonly, strong, nonatomic)
    NSManagedObjectModel
    *managedObjectModel;
    @property (readonly, strong, nonatomic)
    NSPersistentStoreCoordinator
    *persistentStoreCoordinator;
    ```

    These are declared here so that we can access them easily from any screen.

2. Next, we will declare the code for each of the objects in `AppDelegate.m`
    such as the following lines of code that will create an instance of
    `NSManagedObjectContext` and return an existing instance if the instance
    already exists. This is important as you want only one instance of the context
    to be present to avoid conflicting access to the context:

    ```
    - (NSManagedObjectContext *)managedObjectContext
    {
        if (_managedObjectContext != nil) {
            return _managedObjectContext;
        }
        NSPersistentStoreCoordinator *coordinator = [self
        persistentStoreCoordinator];
        if (coordinator != nil) {
            _managedObjectContext = [[NSManagedObjectContext
            alloc] init];
            [_managedObjectContext
            setPersistentStoreCoordinator:coordinator];
        }

        if (_managedObjectContext == nil)
            NSLog(@"_managedObjectContext is nil");
        return _managedObjectContext;
    }
    ```

This method will create the `NSManagedObjectModel` instance and then return the instance, but it will return an existing `NSManagedObjectModel` instance if it already exists:

```
// Returns the managed object model for the application.
- (NSManagedObjectModel *)managedObjectModel
{
    if (_managedObjectModel != nil) {
        return _managedObjectModel;//return model since it
        already exists
    }

    //else create the model and return it
    //CustomerModel is the filename of your *.xcdatamodeld
    file
    NSURL *modelURL = [[NSBundle mainBundle]
    URLForResource:@"CustomerModel" withExtension:@"momd"];
    _managedObjectModel = [[NSManagedObjectModel alloc]
    initWithContentsOfURL:modelURL];

    if (_managedObjectModel == nil)
        NSLog(@"_managedObjectModel is nil");
    return _managedObjectModel;
}
```

This method will create an instance of the `NSPersistentStoreCoordinator` class if it does not exist, and also return an existing instance if it already exists. We will also make some logs appear in our Xcode console using the `NSLog` method to tell the user if the instance of `NSPersistentStoreCoordinator` is nil and use the `NSSQLiteStoreType` keyword to signify to the system that we intend to store the data in a SQLite database:

```
// Returns the persistent store coordinator for the
application.
- (NSPersistentStoreCoordinator
*)persistentStoreCoordinator
{ NSPersistentStoreCoordinator
    if (_persistentStoreCoordinator != nil) {
        return _persistentStoreCoordinator;//return
        persistent store
    }//coordinator since it already exists

    NSURL *storeURL = [[self applicationDocumentsDirectory]
    URLByAppendingPathComponent:@"CustomerModel.sqlite"];
```

```
    NSError *error = nil;
    _persistentStoreCoordinator = [[NSPersistentStoreCoordinator
alloc]
initWithManagedObjectModel:[self managedObjectModel]];

    if (_persistentStoreCoordinator == nil)
        NSLog(@"_persistentStoreCoordinator is nil");

    if (![_persistentStoreCoordinator addPersistentStoreWithTy
pe:NSSQLiteStoreType configuration:nil URL:storeURL options:nil
error:&error]) {
        NSLog(@"Error %@, %@", error, [error userInfo]);
        abort();
    }

    return _persistentStoreCoordinator;
}
```

The following lines of code will return a URL of the location to store your data on the device:

```
#pragma mark - Application's Documents directory// Returns
the URL to the application's Documents directory.
- (NSURL *)applicationDocumentsDirectory
{
    return [[[NSFileManager defaultManager]
    URLsForDirectory:NSDocumentDirectory
inDomains:NSUserDomainMask] lastObject];
}
```

As you can see, what we have done is to check whether the objects such as _managedObjectModel are nil and if they are not nil, then we return the object, or we will create the object and then return it. This concept is exactly the same concept of lazy loading, which we covered in *Chapter 5, Managing Your Application Data*. We apply the same methodology to managedObjectContext and persistentStoreCoordinator. We did this so that we know that we only have one instance of managedObjectModel, managedObjectContext, and persistentStoreCoordinator created and present at any given time. This is to help us avoid having multiple copies of these objects, which will increase the chance of a memory leak.

Note that memory management is still a real issue in the post-ARC world. So what we have done is follow best practices that will help us avoid memory leaks.

In the example code that was shown, we adopted a structure so that only one instance of managedObjectModel, managedObjectContext, and persistentStoreCoordinator is available at any given time.

Next, let's move on to showing you how to store data in our persistent store. As you can see in the preceding screenshot, we have fields such as name, age, address, email, and phone_number, which correspond to the appropriate fields in our Customer entity.

 The example code in this chapter will be provided in its entirety on the Packt Publishing website, and you can download it and run the Xcode project directly.

Saving data into the persistent store

To do a successful save using Core Data, you require:

- NSManagedObject
- NSManagedObjectContext
- NSPersistentStoreCoordinator
- NSManagedObjectModel

So, in our screen that saves these variables into our Customer entity, the following code fragment does all the magic for the (IBAction)save:(id)sender method. This will enable us to save our data from a new customer or update an existing customer's information:

```
- (IBAction)save:(id)sender {
    if ([nameTxtField text].length == 0)
    {
        UIAlertView *alert = [[UIAlertView alloc]
        initWithTitle:@"Error"
                message:@"Name must not be empty" delegate:self
                    cancelButtonTitle:@"OK"
                    otherButtonTitles:nil];
        [alert show];
        return;
    }
    NSString *name = [nameTxtField text];
    NSString *phone = [phoneTxtField text];
    NSString *email = [emailTxtField text];
    NSString *address = [addressTxtField text];
```

```
int age = [[ageTxtField text] intValue];

//save using core data
NSManagedObjectContext *context = nil;
id delegate = [[UIApplication sharedApplication] delegate];
if ([delegate
performSelector:@selector(managedObjectContext)]) {
    context = [delegate managedObjectContext];
}//prepare the context for saving

if (customer)//if we are showing existing customer data
{
    NSNumber *age = [NSNumber numberWithInt:[[ageTxtField
    text] intValue]];
    [customer setValue:[nameTxtField text] forKey:@"name"];
    [customer setValue:age forKey:@"age"];
    [customer setValue:[addressTxtField text]
    forKey:@"address"];
    [customer setValue:[emailTxtField text] forKey:@"email"];
    [customer setValue:[phoneTxtField text]
    forKey:@"phone_number"];
}
else
{
    // Insert new object into the context
    NSManagedObject *newCustomer = [NSEntityDescription
    insertNewObjectForEntityForName:@"Customer"
    inManagedObjectContext:context];
    [newCustomer setValue:name forKey:@"name"];
    [newCustomer setValue:phone forKey:@"phone_number"];
    [newCustomer setValue:email forKey:@"email"];
    [newCustomer setValue:address forKey:@"address"];
    [newCustomer setValue:[NSNumber numberWithInteger:age]
    forKey:@"age"];
}

NSError *error = nil;
// Save the object to persistent store
NSString *str;
if (![context save:&error]) {
    str = [NSString stringWithFormat:@"Error saving %@ with
    localized description %@", error, [error
    localizedDescription]];
    NSLog(@"%@", str);
}
```

```
    else
    {
        str = @"Customer record saved to persistent store";
        if (customer)
            str = @"Customer record updated to persistent store";
        NSLog(@"%@", str);
    }

    UIAlertView *alert = [[UIAlertView alloc]
    initWithTitle:@"Alert"
                                        message:str delegate:self
                            cancelButtonTitle:@"OK"
                            otherButtonTitles:nil];

    [alert show];
}
```

So, the steps we need to remember are:

1. Get the instance of NSManagedObjectContext, which sets persistentStoreCoordinator using managedObjectModel.

2. Create an instance of NSManagedObject and set the values you want to save.

3. Use an object of the NSManagedObjectContext type and call the save method since the context will represent all changes that you have done and you need to call the save method in order to save the changes from the context to disk.

Deleting data from the persistent store

We will now move on to delete a record from the persistent store. In our table view, we will load the customers using an instance of NSFetchRequest, as shown:

```
- (void)viewDidAppear:(BOOL)animated
{
    [super viewDidAppear:animated];

    //Get the context first
    NSManagedObjectContext *managedObjectContext = [self
    managedObjectContext];

    //load data from Customer entity
    NSFetchRequest *fetchRequest = [[NSFetchRequest alloc]
    initWithEntityName:@"Customer"];
```

```
    self.customers = [[managedObjectContext
    executeFetchRequest:fetchRequest error:nil] mutableCopy];


    [tblView reloadData];
}
```

Here, we will declare customers as a mutable array to store our records from the Customer entity:

```
@property (strong) NSMutableArray *customers;
```

To delete a record, we just need to get our Customer record, which is an instance of NSManagedObject from the customers array, then use an instance of managedObjectContext to call the deleteObject method on it, and finally, call the save method to save our updated records:

```
- (void)tableView:(UITableView *)tableView
commitEditingStyle:(UITableViewCellEditingStyle)editingStyle
forRowAtIndexPath:(NSIndexPath *)indexPath
{
    NSManagedObjectContext *context = [self managedObjectContext];

    if (editingStyle == UITableViewCellEditingStyleDelete) {

        NSManagedObject *obj = [self.customers
        objectAtIndex:indexPath.row];
        [context deleteObject: obj];

        NSError *error = nil;
        NSString *str;
        // Attempt to delete record from database
        if (![context save:&error]) {
            str = @"Cannot delete record! %@", [error
            localizedDescription];
            NSLog(@"%@", str);
        }
        else
        {
            // Remove customer from table view
            [self.customers removeObject:obj];

            //update tableview
            [tblView deleteRowsAtIndexPaths:[NSArray
            arrayWithObject:indexPath]

withRowAnimation:UITableViewRowAnimationNone];
```

```
        str = @"Record removed";
        NSLog(@"%@", str);
    }


    UIAlertView *alert = [[UIAlertView alloc]
    initWithTitle:@"Alert"
                                message:str delegate:self
                        cancelButtonTitle:@"OK"
                        otherButtonTitles:nil];


    [alert show];
    }
}
```

Updating data

Finally, to update a record, it is much simpler than you think, thanks to the abstraction layer. To update data, we just assign the values to our customer object in the (IBAction) save: (id) sender method, which you saw earlier:

```
if (customer)//if we showing existing customer data
{
        NSNumber *age = [NSNumber numberWithInt:[[ageTxtField
        text] intValue]];
        [customer setValue:[nameTxtField text] forKey:@"name"];
        [customer setValue:age forKey:@"age"];
        [customer setValue:[addressTxtField text]
        forKey:@"address"];
        [customer setValue:[emailTxtField text] forKey:@"email"];
        [customer setValue:[phoneTxtField text]
        forKey:@"phone_number"];
    }
```

We will add the following code after we set the values of our customer object:

```
NSError *error = nil;
    // Save the object to persistent store
    NSString *str;
    if (![context save:&error]) {
        str = [NSString stringWithFormat:@"Error saving %@ with
        localized description %@", error, [error
        localizedDescription]];
        NSLog(@"%@", str);
    }
```

Here, `customer` is an instance of `NSManagedObject`:

```
@property (strong) NSManagedObject *customer;
```

The code for updating data is to be added after the following code fragment, inside the − `(IBAction)save:(id)sender` method:

```
if ([delegate performSelector:@selector(managedObjectContext)]) {
        context = [delegate managedObjectContext];
    }//prepare the context for saving
```

Summary

So, to wrap it all up, Core Data is not something that is overly complex and the code to use Core Data is pretty straightforward as we have seen in our code examples shown earlier. The Core Data framework is a relatively easy framework to use to handle data storage abstraction without worrying about different data storage formats.

The concepts that you have to know are the Core Data classes such as `NSManagedObject`, `NSManagedObjectContext`, `NSPersistentStoreCoordinator`, and so on and the related methods such as `save` and `deleteObject`. With these simple lines of code, you can leverage the power of the Core Data framework to do data persistence on a high-level abstraction without concerning yourself with the low-level data format specifications.

In the next chapter, we will be introduced to key-value programming and how it can be used to allow us to be notified of state changes. So, I hope you enjoyed this chapter on Core Data!

7
Key-value Programming Approaches

Key-value coding is a really cool function that works well with key-value observing. It allows you to code less and create very elegant solutions and code modules. There are many cases in a real application when something changes and another part of the application should be affected. The thing is that you can do anything when a property of an instance or class changes, including but not limited to checking whether its value is valid, sending a message to someone when something changes to a certain value, and so on. The options are unlimited.

We will cover the following topics in this chapter:

- What is key-value coding?
- The NSKeyValueCoding protocol
- Manual subsets of the NSKeyValueCoding behavior
- Associated objects
- Selectors as keys
- Maximum flexibility and handling unusual keys/values

Also, do note that the NSKeyValueCoding protocol has been available since Mac OS X 10.0 in Cocoa, and it has also made its appearance in iOS 2.0, which came out in July 11, 2008. Generally, APIs for iOS and Mac tend to make their appearance on the Mac platform first before making their appearance on the iOS platform.

What is key-value coding or KVC?

Key-value coding is basically a mechanism to indirectly access an object's properties, rather than explicitly getting and setting those properties via instance variables. With KVC, we use strings as properties keys, which act as an identifier. It is used by passing a "key", which is a string to get or set the property related to that key. For example, take a look at the following code sample:

```
@interface DogClass
@property NSString *dog_name;
@property NSInteger number_legs;
@end

DogClass *mydog = [[DogClass alloc] init];
NSString *string = [myDog valueForKey:@"dog_name"];
[mydog setValue:@4 forKey:@"number_legs"];
```

In the preceding code, we created `DogClass` with two properties of `NSString` and `NSInteger`. Then, we used `valueForKey` and `setValue` to get the value of `dog_name` and `number_legs` respectively using key-value coding.

If this sounds familiar to you, you may recognize the syntactical similarity when using NSDictionary.

There is another sample code, which you can refer to for more clarification. Let's check out the following code:

```
// The following line sets a property, directly.
//Example A
myObject.myProperty = myValue;

/*
  While this other line sets the same property, this time using
  KVC.
*/
//Example B
[myObject setValue:myValue forKey:@"myProperty"];
```

Some developers who were introduced to Objective-C earlier disliked this approach of setting the property explicitly using the dot operator as seen in `myObject.myProperty = myValue`, but it is essentially helpful since it separates the property involved in the setting process from the action of setting itself. A normal setter is applicable in this context, but writing your own setters will mean that you are writing a lot of boilerplate code and this will make your code more verbose.

Basically, your app's accessor methods will implement the methods and patterns signatures determined by the KVC. The task of those accessor methods is to provide a way into the property values of your application's data models. There are two of them, set and get accessors. The set accessors—also known as setters—set the property's value, while the get ones—also known as getters—get/return the property's value.

Imagine a NSTableViewDataSource method to handle an edit for one of the rows, other than the default one, without it being KVC. It should look like the following code:

```
- (void)tableView:(NSTableView *)aTableView
    setMyObjectValue:(NSString *)anObject
    forMyTableColumn:(NSTableColumn *)aTableColumn
    row:(int)rowIndex
{
    if ([[aTableColumn identifier] isEqual:@"myName"])
    {
        [[myRecords objectAtIndex:rowIndex] setName:anObject];
    }
    else if ([[aTableColumn identifier] isEqual:@"myAddress"])
    {
        [[myRecords objectAtIndex:rowIndex] setAddress:anObject];
    }
}
```

However, as soon as we can use KVC, the method can be like this:

```
- (void)tableView:(NSTableView *)aTableView
    setMyObjectValue:(NSString *)anObject
    forMyTableColumn:(NSTableColumn *)aTableColumn
    row:(int)rowIndex
{
    [[myRecords objectAtIndex:rowIndex] setValue:anObject
forKey:[aTableColumn identifier]];
}
```

The essence of KVC is shown here; it's a better approach because each property's edit doesn't need to be handled as a separate condition. Another huge advantage is its efficiency since a table with thousands of columns will be handled by the same code, not even a line added to it. Notice that in the first example, we needed to have two if loops to handle two different identifiers, but using KVC, we can cut down on the verbose code and use setValue instead and achieve the same result with just one statement.

Besides the fact that key-value coding simplifies your code, implementing its compliant accessors is an effective design principle, and it helps the data encapsulation and makes it easier to work with key-value observing — which we will cover later — and other technologies such as Cocoa bindings, Core Data, and so on.

`NSKeyValueCoding` is an informal protocol that provides the essential methods for KVC, while `NSObject` provides its default implementations. Key-value coding can access three types of object values; they are attributes, one-to-one relationships, and one-to-many relationships, where we can access a property indirectly using a string.

What we call attribute is just a simple value property, so it might be a `NSString` or `Boolean` value, as well as `NSNumber` and other immutable object types.

When an object has properties of its own, these are known as properties, which are assigned a one-to-one relationship between the object and property. What is interesting about these properties is that they can change, without the object changing itself at all. To better understand this, think of a `NSView` instance's superview as a one-to-one relationship. A set of related objects make a one-to-many relationship. We can see this in `NSArray` or `NSSet` instances, where a `NSArray` or `NSSet` instance has a one-to-many relationship to a group of objects.

The NSKeyValueCoding protocol

The `NSKeyValueCoding` protocol is used in every sample code I've shown until now. I also have been calling it a protocol, but as I said earlier, it's an informal protocol, a `NSObject` category.

KVC is a mechanism that enables you to indirectly access an object's properties, using a "key" of strings to do it. To enable KVC, `NSKeyValueCoding` must be complied by your classes. Most of the time, you don't need to do anything in order to get it done because it's complied by `NSObject`.

To make a key-value coding compliant class for a certain property, the methods `setValue:forKey:` and `valueForKey:` must be implemented to work as expected.

Compliance of attributes and one-to-one relationships

You must ensure that your class has the following specification in case the of properties that are simply attributes or one-to-one relationships; an example would be `[myObject setValue:myValue forKey:@"myProperty"];`, which we saw earlier:

- Have an instance variable called `<key>` or `_<key>`, or have an implemented method called `-<key>`, which is a reference to the key in your key-value pair. As a rule of thumb, KVC keys start with lowercase letters, but for ones, such as URL, it's also acceptable if the first letter is uppercase.

- If the property is a mutable one, `-set<Ket>:` would be also implemented.

- The implementation of the `-set<Key>:` method should not include any validation as validation is to be implemented by the method mentioned in the next point.

- If the validation is suitable for the key, `-validate<Key>:error:` must be implemented here along with your validation code.

Compliance of indexed one-to-many relationships

Using `NSArrays` or `NSMutableArrays` will introduce you to the concept of one to-many relationships, where the key-value coding compliance requirements for indexed to-many relationships you need to ensure are:

- The implementation of a method called `-<key>`, returning an array

- Besides, you might have an `NSArray` instance variable called `<key>` or `_<key>` or even proceed the implementation of `-countOf<Key>` and one or all of the following: `-<key>AtIndexes:` or `-objectIn<Key>AtIndex:`

- In order to improve performance, you can also implement `-get<Key>:range:` but it's not a requirement

Otherwise, if you are dealing with mutable indexed ordered one to-many relationships, these are your requirements:

- Get at least one of the methods implemented:
  `-insertObject:in<Key>AtIndex:` and `-insert<Key>:atIndexes:`

- Get at least one of the methods implemented:
  `-removeObjectFrom<Key>AtIndex:` and `-remove<Key>AtIndexes:`

- As an option, you can even implement one of the methods:
  `-replace<Key>AtIndexes:with` or `-replaceObjectIn<Key>AtIndex:with Object:`

Compliance of unordered many-to-many relationships

NSSets are an example of an unordered collection and also have a many to-many relationship, so the key-value coding compliance requirements for unordered many to-many relationships you need to ensure are:

- The implementation of a method called `-<key>`, returning an `NSSet`
- Otherwise, set an instance variable called `<key>` or `_<key>`
- Or get these methods implemented: `-enumeratorOf<Key>`, `-countOf<Key>`, and `-memberOf<Key>:`

If it's a mutable unordered to-many relationship, KVC compliance will ask you to:

- Implement at least one of the following methods: `-add<Key>:` or `-add<Key>Object:`
- Implement at least one of the following methods: `-remove<Key>:` or `-remove<Key>Object:`
- In order to improve performance, you can implement `-set<Key>:` and `-insert<Key>:`

With NSString keys, you can set and get values using the methods `setValue:forKey:` and `valueForKey:`. This key is a simple string that serves as an identifier to an object's property. A key must be in accordance with the following rules: starting with a lowercase letter, shouldn't contain white-spaces, and make use of ASCII encoding. All these rules are applied in the following sample keys: `mySampleKey`, `pageNumber`, and `oddSum`.

There are also key paths, they're basically a string with two or more keys separated by dots, as `pictures.byOwner.forYear`. If you have a hard time trying to understand, think about it as a UNIX directory relative path as shown here, `pictures/Vasilkoff/2014`.

It's clear that the folder 2014 is relative to `Vasilkoff`, which is relative to `pictures`, which in turn is relative to the user's current directory. In key paths, the first key — in our preceding code sample: `pictures` — is relative to the receiver object.

For example, using the concept of address and street as you can derive a street from the address. So, if you use the same concept, the `address.street` key path will get the value of the address property from the receiving object, and then you can determine the street property relative to the address object.

Advantages of key-value coding

- Most properties support the NSKeyValueCoding informal protocol by default. Any object that inherits from NSObject has automatic support for NSKeyValueCoding. So, your own custom class will not have support for NSKeyValueCoding unless you explicitly make it inherit from NSObject.

- KVC will automatically look for setter and getter methods and if none is found, then it will even get or set instance variables.

- The possibility of using key paths is really helpful while handling multiple property objects.

- To be notified of the state change, KVC can be easily integrated with NSKeyValueObserving in order to implement the observer software pattern.

- The possibility of dealing with undefined keys.

- This provides fallbacks.

Disadvantages of key-value coding

- The property keys must be only NSStrings, which means that the compiler does not have any information on the type of property or any details about its existence. So, any type of information cannot be retrieved from the return value of ID, which as you know, is a pointer to an Objective-C object.

- Its extended search path makes it a very slow KVC approach.

- The class must provide a method or an instance variable matching the name of the property, only then it will be found by NSKeyValueCoding. If there is a typo in your key, your application will crash during runtime and not compile time, so you must make sure that your key is spelled correctly to avoid a crash.

Manual subsets of NSKeyValueCoding behavior

The NSKeyValueCoding protocol acts in different ways while looking up for methods and instance variables. In the first case, it will look up for the method's selector's name, while in the last, it will look up for the instance variable's name.

This can be done manually, as we can see in the following samples:

```
// Manual implementation of KVC setter for method.
NSString *mySetterString = [@"set"
stringByAppendingString:[myKeyString capitalizedString]];
[myObject performSelector:NSSelectorFromString(mySetterString)
withObject:myValue];

// Manual implementation of KVC setter for instance variable.
object_setInstanceVariable(myObject, myKeyString, myValue);
```

Since KVC can look up for setters and getters automatically, you might only be required to use the preceding approach by creating your own lookup path if you want to avoid NSKeyValueCoding to find specified or ordinary methods and instance variables.

Advantages of creating your own lookup path

To avoid NSKeyValueCoding, looking for methods or instance variables that will normally be found by NSKeyValueCoding and creating your own lookup path will be the approach you require. Let's start with the advantages and follow that up with the disadvantages:

- It may be faster than normal NSKeyValueCoding paths.
- It gives you more control over the path. Unlike NSKeyValueCoding paths, it will also work for non NSObject inherited classes.
- By doing it manually, non-object values can be used for get and set.

Disadvantages of creating your own lookup path

- Generally, you will spend more time working on it than just using normal NSKeyValueCoding paths
- It also provides less flexibility as you need to write more code to cover any unusual key/value cases, which is normally covered by the automatic method

Associated objects

In the Objective-C 2.0 runtime used by apps in iOS and 64-bit Mac OS X, you're allowed to set an association from any object to another. The object, in this case, without support from instance variables or methods can have a random set of extra properties set by the key at runtime, shown as follows:

```
objc_setAssociatedObject(myObject, myKey, myValue,
OBJC_ASSOCIATION_RETAIN_NONATOMIC);
```

You can use this if you want to set a property from outside an object. If you would be an object and your t-shirt color a property of yours, it would be like someone changing its color from outside your house, and you wouldn't even notice it.

You should use it in similar circumstances, where you want to keep the object away for knowing, supporting, or being involved while you set a property from other parts of the program. Associated objects should not be the method you want to use at the top of your head as lack of type information makes it easy for a crash to appear due to incorrect typing.

Advantages of using associated objects

- A key can be any pointer. In this case, OBJC_ASSOCIATION_ASSIGN can be used.
- It may be the fastest key-value coding approach.
- There is no support required from the method or instance variable.

Disadvantages of using associated objects

- It has no effect over the object itself (instance variable or method). The object won't know about its own changes.
- In associated objects, a key is no longer NSString, but a pointer.

Selectors as keys

Normally, KVC looks up for a property key and acts only after the property key is found. The other approach is about acting on an object's property in the lookup process. There is a lookup method in Objective-C core and its keys are used as selectors.

The following line of code is how you implement this lookup method:

```
objc_msgSend(myObject, mySetterSelector, myValue);
```

 This method is very similar to the manual implementation of the instance variable's setter, but instead of using the key to form a selector to do a look up, it uses the selector itself as the key.

Advantages of using selectors as keys

- It's possible to get and set non-object data.
- From all approaches that handles methods, this is the fastest one.

Disadvantages of using selectors as keys

- You need different selectors for get and set
- Since selectors are not objects, it's impossible to store directly in NSArray and NSDictionary. Instead, you can use NSValue or Core Foundation

Maximum flexibility and handling unusual keys/values

After you learned so many ways to use key-value coding, there is still a very important way of implementation if you are looking for more flexibility while handling unusual keys/values. Just do it yourself. The final approach to key-value coding is to handle the implementation yourself.

Create a getter and setter method, and inside of each method properly returning and setting the values on a dictionary owned by the object might be the easiest way to do it.

We can check out this approach in the following sample code:

```
/*
//-----------------------------
  We create the method called "setCollectionValue:forKey:"
//-----------------------------
*/
```

```objc
- (void) setCollectionValue: (id) value forKey: (NSString *) key
{
    /*
    //-----------------------------
    Here we set the value for key in a dictionary
    owned by the object.
    //-----------------------------
    */

    [collectionDictionary setObject:value forKey:key];
}

/*
//-----------------------------
    Then, we create the method called "getCollectionValueForKey:"
    Note that it's a getter method, so it must return
    something - (id)
//-----------------------------
*/
- (id) getCollectionValueForKey: (NSString *) key
{
    /*
    //-----------------------------
    Here, we get the object from the dictionary, for the
    specified key and return it.
    //-----------------------------
    */

    return [collectionDictionary objectForKey:key];
}
```

In our sample code, we used `NSDictionary` for the value's internal storage; however, you can use your own storage solutions, or even Cocoa key-value storage structures:

- `NSMutableDictionary`
- `NSMapTable`
- `CFMutableDictionaryRef`

Advantages of doing your own implementation

- Multiple collections can be exposed by a single object
- Any data type supported by the respective collection can be used while getting and setting
- Among all methods of implementation, this is the most flexible one

Disadvantages of doing your own implementation

- It simply does not work for random objects, only the target class
- You're unable to use other `NSKeyValueCoding` concepts in addition to this

Key-value observing

Key-value observing—also known as KVO—is a way to get notified about changes in a variable, but only if it was changed using KVC. We can highlight two things out of this:

- Firstly, you need KVC in order to do KVO
- Secondly, if a variable is changed directly without key-value coding by its default setter and getter methods, you won't get notified at all

Every variable in any key path can be observed by an object. It's useful if you consider using KVO. As KVO is built on top of KVC, you need KVC to implement KVO, and using KVO should be one of the reasons why you need to use KVC.

Implementing key-value observing

It is relatively easy to implement KVO, as we shall see in the following code example. On the specified key path, you add an observer. After this, you can create a method that will be called anytime the observer sees modifications in the variables on its key path.

An object can be registered as an observer by using the following method from `NSKeyCodingProtocol`: `addObserver:forKeyPath:options:context:`. Anytime a modification is performed, the following method is called `observeValueForKeyPath :ofObject:change:context:`.

Firstly, go to your class and add the following method:

```
-(void)observeValueForKeyPath:(NSString *)keyPath
ofObject:(id)object change:(NSDictionary *)change context:(void
*)context
{
}
```

As you saw earlier, this method is called when any modification is performed. However, the protocol is even more powerful than this; it gives you the possibility to be notified about a change before it occurs and also after it's done, by using the respective methods: `willChangeValueForKey` and `didChangeValueForKey`. You might consider these methods if you need time-specific notifications.

Let's check out the following code where we register an object as an observer:

```
/*
//----------------------------
    We register the object "developmentManager" as the
    observer of "developer".
    It will then notify you when any change will take
    place for the key path "developmentStage".
//----------------------------
*/
[developer addObserver:developmentManager
forKeyPath:@"developmentStage"
options:NSKeyValueObservingOptionNew |
NSKeyValueObservingOptionOld context:nil];
```

If you look carefully, you will notice that we've used the options `NSKeyValueObservingOptionNew` and `NSKeyValueObservingOptionOld`. Both are used if we want to know the old and new values. These values will be stored in our dictionary of changes.

In our example, let's assume that development stages are represented by levels, `NSInteger` values from 0 to 10, and at every modification, we need to inform our progress. In this case, we will create two simple methods to do it for us:

```
- (void)informNoProgress
{
  NSLog(@"We had no progress today");
}

- (void)informRealProgress
{
  NSLog(@"Our today's progress is of %@ level",
  developer.developmentStage);
}
```

The two preceding methods are now complete; one will inform no progress if the development stage doesn't change—we will consider that it's impossible to decrease, in our scenario, and the other one will inform the real progress by levels if the development stage changes. However, now, we want to call the properly methods after comparing the values. Remember we used the options NSKeyValueObservingOptionNew and NSKeyValueObservingOptionOld; they will save the old and the new values after a change.

The old and new values will be handled inside the method that is called when the observer notifies a modification, as follows:

```
- (void) observeValueForKeyPath: (NSString *) keyPath
ofObject: (id) object change: (NSDictionary *) change context: (void
*) context
{
    if([keyPath isEqualToString:@"developmentStage"])
    {
    /*
    //-----------------------------
        Here we store the old and new values for
        further comparison.
    //-----------------------------
    */
     NSInteger oldStage = [change
       objectForKey:NSKeyValueChangeOldKey];
    NSInteger newStage = [change
       objectForKey:NSKeyValueChangeNewKey];

    /*
    //-----------------------------
        Then, we check whether the oldStage level is lower
        than the newStage level
    //-----------------------------
    */
     if(oldStage < newStage)
    {
      /*
      //-----------------------------
          If the value is lower, there is progress
          and we call the properly method to inform it
      //-----------------------------
      */
       [self informRealProgress];

    } else {
```

```
/*
//-----------------------------
    However, if the old level is not lower, it
    means there was no progress, we call the
    method to inform it.
//-----------------------------
*/
  [self informNoProgress];
}
    }
}
```

In the preceding code, we make sure that if the observed key is the one we are actually looking for, just to be really sure—in our case, the key is `developmentStage`. Then, we store the old and the new values in order to compare them. If there are positive changes, inform the progress, if not, call the other method to inform about the bad news.

This is a real handy tool, even more if it is used cleverly as it is really powerful since it allows us to observe or watch a KVC key path on an object and to be notified when the value of the object changes, which can be useful in some programming contexts. Having control even on the change of your properties is a really powerful feature, and I'm sure you will find great cases to use in your own projects.

Performance considerations

You must be careful while overriding KVC methods implementation as the default implementation caches Objective-C runtime information in order to be more effective and less erroneous, and unnecessary overriding implementations can affect the performance of your application.

Summary

So far, we have taken a deep dive into key-value coding and other details such as various implementation methods, their advantages and disadvantages, and also key-value observing—a mechanism built on top of key-value coding.

We also saw some working code for key-value coding and key-value observing with some explanation on why we prefer to use key-value coding over other similar methods such as using a dot operator to access properties.

With this, I hope all these will help to give you an understanding of key-value coding and key-value observing. So with this, let's move on to the next chapter where we will wade into the brand new language by Apple called Swift.

8
Introduction to Swift

Apple held their **Worldwide Developers Conference (WWDC)** for 2014 on June 2 at Moscone West in San Francisco, which was the same venue as previous years. They announced a slew of new APIs, technologies for games such as Metal, new operating systems for iOS (iOS 8) and Mac (Yosemite), and the most important announcement for iOS developers in 2014, that is, the announcement of Swift, a new programming language, which some say is meant to replace Objective-C, as Objective-C was introduced in 1983 and is showing its age due to its long history. Swift is meant to be an easy and simple to learn programming language that will lower the barrier to entry for developers who are intimidated by Objective-C. However, what is Swift and what is good about it? How far does it differ from Objective-C, and finally, how easy is it to learn Swift? These are the questions that we will cover in this chapter, and to start things off, here is a list of topics we will cover:

- Welcome to Swift
- Swift basics
- Memory management

Welcome to Swift

Swift is actually not a new language, as Apple started the development of Swift back in 2010. Since programming languages such as Ruby, Python, Haskell, Rust, and so on have surged in popularity, Swift was developed using language ideas from these popular languages. As Apple describes Swift as *Objective-C without the C*, you can consider Swift as a language that is a reimagining of Objective-C using modern concepts and syntax borrowed from languages such as JavaScript, but still keeping the essence and spirit of Objective-C.

Swift does away with pointers and makes memory management opaque to the developer through the use of ARC so that they can focus on their iOS application creation and not worry about memory management most of the time. Swift uses ARC and not the GC method found in Java. This means that Swift can still leak memory if you are not careful by using cyclic strong references. Smalltalk is a programming language released in 1972 that has heavily influenced Objective-C in terms of architecture, such as message passing. And the Smalltalk aspect of Objective-C, such as method calls, has been replaced with dot notation and a namespace system that is reminiscent of Java and C#. However, Swift is not a totally radical departure from Objective-C. Key Objective-C concepts such as protocols, closures, and categories are still present in Swift, except that the syntax is much cleaner and crisper.

Swift's approach to memory management is that it uses ARC, and one problem with ARC is that a developer can unintentionally create a strong reference cycle where instances of two different classes include a reference to the other. So, Swift provides the weak and unowned keyboards to prevent strong reference cycles from occurring.

For a seasoned Objective-C programmer who comes from a C or C++ background, Swift may seem like a totally new language as it does away with some aspects of Objective-C such as verbosity. I am sure that a lot of Objective-C developers have experienced "square brackets hell", where simple functionalities need to be wrapped with a lot of square brackets, thus rendering the code hard to read, and which also runs the risk of introducing bugs into your application. The goal of Swift is to let developers harness the power of Objective-C without C. So, there are some aspects of Swift that indeed make it easier for a developer, but conversely, there are some parts of Swift that do not seem to be fully fleshed out yet. However, bear in mind that at the time of writing this, Swift is still in beta and Apple may still introduce a lot of changes in the following weeks and months. However, with Apple putting its full weight behind Swift, now is a good time to start learning some Swift basics. As with all new technology that Apple introduces, you will require Xcode 6 beta and higher to run and build your Swift code as Xcode 5 does not support Swift. Your Swift code can also run on iOS 7 and Mac OS 10.9.3. So, if you are an Apple developer, you can download Xcode 6 beta and install it on your Mac as it will be installed side by side with your Xcode 5 and will not override anything or break your current Xcode projects. So, let's get cracking.

Basics of Swift

Swift syntax is very different to Objective-C, while Objective-C has a lot of reliance on C and C++ components such as pointers, strong typing, and so on. Swift is very similar to popular scripting languages such as Python and Ruby with regards to terseness and variable declaration. So, let's look at some basics of Swift to get acquainted with it.

Variable declaration

Swift does away with the need to remember ints, floats, NSStrings, and so on and consolidates all of these type of variables under one type, and that is of the type `var`. If you are familiar with JavaScript, then the `var` keyword should not be unfamiliar to you. Swift supports the type inference, where depending on the value that you assign to a variable, it will infer its type:

```
var welcome
welcome = "Hello world"
```

This means that the variable, `welcome`, is inferred to have a string type as I assigned the text `Hello world` to it. However, if you want to be specific, you can annotate a variable like this:

```
var welcome: String.
```

Then to append two strings together in Swift, you can do the following:

```
welcome += " Bob"
```

If you were using Objective-C, you will need to type out the longer syntax:

```
NSString *hello = @"Hello world";
str = [str stringByAppendingString:@" Bob];
```

Swift also supports constants with the keyword `let`. So, to declare a constant, you can just type the following syntax:

```
let LIFE_MEANING = 42
```

Note that Swift now infers that `LIFE_MEANING` is an integer as you have assigned the value `42` to it. To print out a line of text for logging, which is analogous to NSLog from Apple's Cocoa framework, you can use the `println` keyword, whereas with NSLog, you need to specify the format specifier such as `%d` for integers, `%@` for NSStrings, or `%f` for float/double.

There is no need to do this for Swift; you can just use the following syntactical examples:

```
println("The text is \(welcome)") //print out the value of
variable welcome
println("The meaning of life is \(LIFE_MEANING)")//print out the
meaning of life
```

One thing that has not changed from Objective-C is that comments in Swift are denoted by the // for single line comments and /* and */ for multiline comments.

Semicolons are also optional. Some of you may want to be pedantic and put a semicolon, but personally, I don't like any additional typing than is necessary, so I tend to omit the semicolon (;) for my Swift code.

```
The text is Bob
The meaning of life is 42
```

As with all programming languages, Swift supports an array of operators for arithmetic comparison and assignment.

All the operators such as /, *, +, and so on perform the same function as in Objective-C except that the + operator serves a dual function as a string concatenation operator if you need to concatenate multiple strings.

Swift introduces the concept of closed range operators, which defines a range that runs from x to y and includes the values x and y if you use it like this $(x...y)$. For example:

```
for index in 1...5 {
   print("Value is \(index)")
}
```

This will print out the values **1**, **2**, **3**, **4**, and **5**. As you may have noticed by now, this can be used to replace the more verbose tradition for loop in Objective-C, which is represented by these lines of code:

```
for (int i = 0; i <= 5, i ++)
NSLog(@"Value is %d", i);
```

However, what if you want to do some common `for` loop code to loop through an array? Then, you will need a half-closed range operator, which is similar to a closed range operator except that there is one dot less (*x..y*):

```
let breeds = ["Pitbull", "Terrier", Bull dog", "Maltese"]
let count = breeds.count
for i in 0..count {
  println("This breed is \(breeds[i])")
}
```

As you have seen earlier, Swift also has support for collection types such as arrays as shown earlier and dictionaries, which we will cover in the next few pages. To start off declaring an array, you just use the following syntax:

```
var catBreeds = ["Siamese", "Scottish"]
```

Then, there are some properties that can come in handy, among others, such as:

- `count`: This returns the number of items in the array
- `isEmpty`: This is a Boolean variable that returns true if the count property is 0
- `append`: This property will allow you to add an item to the end of an array

Swift provides some helper code to iterating over an array instead of using a `for` loop, `while` loop, or `do-while` loop. Array iteration is easier in Swift as you just need to do this to do the iteration:

```
for item in catBreeds{
  println(item)
}//prints out "Siamese" and "Scottish"
```

No longer do you need to write any verbose and unnecessary code for a `for`, `while`, or `do-while` loop as you can use the item variable to access the array.

Next, we will cover dictionary. The dictionary in Swift is similar to `NSDictionary` in Cocoa, in terms of functionality and usage. However, there is a major difference in that, whereas in `NSDictionary` and `NSMutableDictionary`, you are allowed to use any object as the key and value, which does not provide any information about the object nature. In Swift, the type of keys and values in a dictionary are always made explicitly clear using explicit type annotation or via type inference.

The syntax for a dictionary in Swift is quite straightforward, as shown here:

```
var breeds = Dictionary<String, String> = ["Breed1": "Bull Dog",
"Breed2": "Terrier"]
```

The preceding code uses explicit type notation as you can see that the key and value are explicitly defined as String and String respectively. This is very similar to how you declare dictionaries in Javascript or Maps in Java, by running the following:

```
var breeds = ["Breed1": "Bull Dog", "Breed2": "Terrier"]
```

The preceding code uses type inference where once we assign Breed1 to the key and Bull Dog to the value, Swift automatically infers that our dictionary will hold two strings.

Modifying a dictionary in Swift is similar to how you access an array except that instead of using an index, you use the key, which in our case is a String. So, if you want to modify the value that maps to the Breed1 key, you can do it as shown here:

```
breeds["Breed1"] = "Dalmatian"
```

Alternatively, Swift allows us to update a value another way, which is the updateValue method as demonstrated here:

```
breeds.updateValue("Breed2", forKey: "Bloodhound")
```

Both ways will allow you to update a value using the key, but I prefer the first way as it is less verbose, yet equally easy to read and understand.

Iteration over a dictionary is similar to the iteration of an array in Swift where we can forgo the old Objective-C for, while, or do-while loop methods. To do a dictionary iteration in Swift, we just use the following code:

```
for (breed, breedname) in breeds{
    println("\(breed) is \(breedname)")
}//prints Breed1 is Dalmation, Breed2 is Bloodhound
```

In any general purpose programming language, control flow statements are a necessity in order to control the flow of your code and your app. So, although Swift is a big departure from Objective-C, it still allows for control flow constructs of C-like languages such as C++.

Here is a list of control flow constructs available for you to use in Swift:

- The for loop
- The for-in loop
- The while loop
- The do-while loop
- The if statement
- The switch statement

These control flow statements serve the same purpose as they will in Objective-C, but there are a few improvements to them, which I will explain briefly.

Iterating statements

For statements that iterate over and over again, such as `for` loops, Swift emphasizes the `for-in` loop for iteration. This is also known as an enhanced for loop in other programming languages such as Java. This improves readability and adds terseness to your code. For example:

```
var dogs = ["Bulldog", "Terrier", "Dalmatian"]
for dog in dogs {
  println("This dog is a \(dog)");
}
```

However, if you have the need for a Objective-C traditional style `for` loop, you can do it with Swift, as follows:

```
for index = 0; index < 3; ++index {
//do something here
}
```

Conditional statements

If statements behave the same way as they do in Objective-C, except for a minor change of syntax as shown here. Do note that the brackets are optional, so we did not put it around the conditional expression:

```
if temperatureInCelsius < 10 {
  println("It is cold here");
}
```

Note that in the preceding example, we have a very simple condition, so we have opted to eliminate our brackets. However, what if you have multiple conditions? Then, Swift will use the normal rules of precedence that you are familiar with, but the lack of brackets can make the operations hard to understand. So, in this case, I would prefer to use brackets for multiple conditions and operations like the following:

```
if (temperatureInCelsius < 10) && (temperatureinCelsius > 0)
{
  println("It is chilly here");
}
```

However, in Swift, Switch statements have now been made easier for debugging by not having to fall through the next case. So now the entire switch statement finishes its execution as soon as the first matching switch case is completed. So, the following statement will show the following output:

```
let number = 2
switch number {
  case 1:
    println("Number is 1");
  case 2:
    println("Number is 2");
  case 3:
    println("Number is 3");
}
```

The output will be `"Number is 2"` in Swift instead of `"Number is 1"` and `"Number is 3"`, which you will see in Objective-C.

Control flows in Swift have been made better where the syntax has been improved to add readability and to prevent developers from creating non-obvious bugs such as a Switch case fallthrough due to a missing `break` statement.

Functions

Functions are the fundamental building blocks of every programming language, and it is also the same in Swift, but there are some improvements made, which we will go through now. The syntax for a function has changed quite a bit, so a function in Swift now has the following syntax:

```
func animalType(animalName: String) -> String {
  let text = "This is a " + animalName
  return text;
}
```

So, you can call it using `println(animalType("Dog"))`. If the function does not have a return value, you can avoid adding the arrow (`->`) like this:

```
func animalType(animalName: String) {
  println("This is a \(animalName)")
}
```

Functions in Swift can now have multiple return values as part of a compound return value where you can use a tuple return type.

A tuple type is just a fancy term for a comma separated list of zero or types, which are enclosed in a parenthesis. So, to let a function have multiple return values, a tuple is what you need as shown here:

```
func myFunc(iCount: Int) -> (intA: Int, intB: int) {
   var intX = 1, intY = 2
   intA = iCount + intX
   intB = iCount + intY
   return (intA, intB)
}
```

Then to use the return value, you need to assign it to a variable:

```
let num = myFunction(10)
println("Value is \(num.intA) and \(num.intB)")
```

Swift allows the default values in a function where a default value is used if a function parameter is not used:

```
func add(num1: Int, num2: Int = 0)
{
   var total = num1 + num2
}
```

So, in the preceding example, `num2` will have a default value of 0 if you do not pass in a parameter for the second parameter in the add function, as shown here:

```
add(1)
```

Swift functions also allow the function to accept a variable number of arguments, which is useful when you need to pass in a varying number of parameters to a function. To enable a function to accept a varying number of parameters, you just need to add three full stops (. . .) in your function, shown as follows:

```
func getAverage(numbers: Double...) -> Double

{
   var total: Double = 0
   for num in numbers {
      total += num
   }

   total = total&/Double(num.count)
   return total
}
```

So, you can call the `getAverage` function using a varying number of parameters such as `getAverage(1, 2, 3)` or `getAverage(1, 2, 3, 4, 5)`. By default, Swift makes all function parameters as constant to promote good programming practice. This is one of the more unique features of Swift, which you do not find in other procedural programming languages such as C++, Objective-C, and so on. So trying to modify a function parameter will result in an error. However, if you need to modify a function parameter in your code, you just need to add the `var` keyword to tell Swift to treat that function parameter as a variable, not as a constant, shown as follows:

```
//num is now a variable and can be modified inside the function
myFunction
func myFunction(var num: Int)
{
}
```

One of the important changes that functions in Swift, different from Objective-C, is that you can have nested functions where a function is created inside another function. But do note that the inner function is only available to the enclosing function. To declare a nested function, you can just use a normal function call:

```
func adder(num: Int)
{
    func addOne(number: Int) -> Int   { return number + 1 }
}
```

Classes and structures in Swift

As you know, classes and structures are general purpose data structures that form the building block of the code of your application. You can define properties and methods to add functionality to these classes and structures using the same syntax as you will for the variables, functions, and so on.

Classes and structures in Swift have many common points such as:

- Defining properties to store values
- Defining methods to provide added functionalities
- The ability to be extended to expand their functionalities
- The possibility to conform to protocols to provide standard functionalities

However, classes have other differences that structures do not possess; they are:

- Inheritance to allow a subclass to inherit the characteristic of another
- Type casting, which allows you to check and interpret the type of a class instance during runtime

- Reference counting, which allows more than one reference to a class instance
- Deinitializers, which allow a class to do resource freeing
- Structures are copied when they are passed around in your code

To declare a class or structure, use the `class` and `struct` keyword respectively:

```
class myClass {
   var x = 0
   var y = 0
}

struct myStruct {
   var x = 0
   var y = 0
}
```

As in Objective-C, to use a `struct` or `class`, you need to create an instance of it before you can use it. So, for `struct` and `class`, you need to use the `()` to create an instance of a `class` or `struct`.

```
let classA = myClass()//creating an instance of a class
let structB = myStruc()//creating an instance of a struct
```

To access a property in a `class` or `struct`, you can use the `"."` operator to access it, as shown here:

```
var myX = classA.x
var myY = structB.y
```

For classes, you can define your own custom initializer and deinitializer in your class file. Initializers for your struct members are automatically created for you, which you can use, as shown here:

```
let yourStruct = myStruct(x: 50, y: 80)
```

Generally, you do not need to do any manual cleanup of your allocated instances as Swift will do it for you using ARC. However, if you are using some custom resources, then you may need to do the additional cleanup yourself. One use case will be when you have a class that opens a text file and writes or appends some data to it. So, in this situation, you may need to close the file before your instance is deallocated. An example syntax of deinitialization is as follows:

```
deinit{
//Your deinitialization code here which could be closing an open
file etc
}
```

One of the most important differences between a Swift class and Swift struct is that Swift classes are passed by reference, which means that a reference to the existing class instance is created when you assign it to another instance, and any change to the new instance will affect the original instance. This is in contrast with pass by value where a copy of the value is passed to the variable so that what happens in the new variable will not affect the original variable.

So, depending on this difference, sometimes using a class is more useful in some situations while in other situations using a struct would be better. It all depends on the context of your program or application. So, let's use some code to help us understand this better:

```
classA = myClass()
classA.x = 80
classB = classA
classB.x = 100
```

If you use the following code, you will notice that the classA member x will also be set to the value of 100 as a reference to classA is passed when you run the code classB = classA. So, whatever affects classB will also affect classA.

Closures

Closures in Swift are known as blocks in Objective-C. Both have the same concept of creating self-contained blocks of code that can be passed around and used.

Closures use { and } to denote the beginning and end respectively. So, a very simple example of creating a closure and calling it would be something like this:

```
var name = "Gibson"
    var greet = {  println("Hello \(name)")    }
    greet()
```

You can see the output **Hello Gibson** appearing in your debug console.

Of course, you will need to pass in arguments and get return values from your closures. You also need to use (and) to enclose your arguments and -> to denote your return values as you can see here:

```
var s1: String = "Howdy"
    var name: String = "Gibby"
    var holler = { (s1: String, name: String) -> String in
        return s1 + " " + name
    }
    var ret = holler(s1, name)
    println(ret)
```

If you run the code, you will get the output **Howdy Gibby** because I passed in two string variables of the names s1 and name respectively as you can see from the line (s1: String, name: String), while I ask a return value of the type string using -> String.

Next, let's move on to memory management in Swift, which you still need to take note of as ARC frees you from a lot of memory management techniques, but you still need to take note of some memory management techniques in Swift as Swift can still leak memory if you are not careful.

Memory management in Swift

Swift was created to avoid some of the downsides of C, one of which being memory management. Notice that nowhere in this chapter did I mention anything about pointers, memory allocation, deallocation, and so on. This is because in Swift, memory management is made to be as painless as possible so that you, the developer, can focus more on your application development than on debugging memory leaks. Every time a new instance of a class is created, ARC will allocate a chunk of the memory to be used to store information about that instance. This chunk of memory holds information such as the instance type (string, integer, and so on) along with the values of the properties that are associated with that instance. ARC will free up the memory used by that instance when it is no longer needed or referenced. This is to avoid a situation where instances still occupy precious memory space when they are no longer being used or needed.

However, if you try to access an instance's properties or methods after ARC has deallocated it, then a crash will be the likely result that you will see. So, to make sure that this does not happen to you, ARC will track how many properties, variables, and constants are currently referencing a class instance, and ARC will not allow deallocation as long as there is at least one active reference to that instance from another object in your code somewhere. A strong reference is created when you assign a class instance to a property, constant, or variable, and this strong reference keeps a strong hold on that class instance, and ARC will not make a deallocation call as long as that strong reference remains. Let's illustrate this with some code to understand this further:

1. Let's declare a class called Dog:

```
class Dog {
  let type: String
  init(_type: String) {
    self.type = _type
    println("Init done")
  }
}
```

```
  deinit {
    println("Deinit done")
  }
}
```

2. Then, we will create two references to the `Dog` class:

```
var dog1: Dog?
Var dog2: Dog?
```

 Note that there is a ? keyword, which means that dog1 is of an optional type, which means that it could be nil. In Swift, any variable with a ? keyword means that there is a possibility that it can hold a nil value. Since we declared dog1 and dog2 as an optional type, it means that dog1 and dog2 are initialized with a value of nil and do not have a reference to the Dog class.

3. Next, we will create an instance and assign two variables, `dog1` and `dog2` respectively:

```
dog1 = Dog(type: "Bulldog")
dog2 = dog1//1 strong reference to dog1 is created
```

So, now there are two strong references to the `Dog` instance. One is through `dog1` and the other is from `dog2` to `dog1`.

One thing to note about Swift is that the type inference only works for the initial assignment; assigning another type to the same variable will throw an error. This is quite different from other languages such as JavaScript, where no error will be thrown. Let me illustrate what I mean with an example:

```
var hello = "Hello World"//this means hello is inferred to
have a type of string
hello = 42
//This will throw an error as now you are assigning an
integer to a string variable
```

4. So, you can try assigning `dog1` to nil, as shown here:

```
dog1 = nil
```

ARC will see that `dog2` still holds a strong reference and will not deallocate the `Dog` instance. The only time that the `Dog` instance will be deallocated will be when `dog2` is set to nil as shown here:

```
dog2 = nil //this will let ARC deallocate the Dog instance
```

Conversely, Swift also supports weak references where the reference does not have a strong reference onto the instance that it references. So, ARC will dispose of an instance even if it has a weak reference. To create a weak reference, you need to use the weak keyword as shown here:

```
weak var cat: String?
```

Notice that the ? keyword is added at the end of the String keyword as a weak reference can be allowed to have a value of nil, so all weak references must be declared as optional using the ? keyword. Notice that it is also declared as a variable as weak references will have their values changed in the code during runtime. So, a weak reference cannot be declared as a constant as a weak reference does not have a strong hold on the instance it refers to. So, when this instance is going to be deallocated while the weak reference is still referring to it, ARC will set the weak reference to nil when that situation arises and you can check the value of a weak reference to see if that object has been deallocated. This way you can avoid a situation where you end up with a reference to an invalid instance that has already been deallocated by ARC.

In between strong and weak references, there is another type of reference that keeps a weak hold on an instance it refers to, but it cannot be set to nil, so it is always assumed to have a value. This is known as an unowned reference. It can be used as a replacement for a weak reference and for some use cases as we will see here:

```
class Country {
  let name: String
  let capital: City!
  init(name: String, capital: String) {
    self.name = name
    self.capital = City(name: name, country: self)
  }

class City {
  let name: String
  unowned let country: Country
  init(name: String, country: Country) {
    self.name = name
    self.country = country
  }
}
```

Notice that we initialize `City` within the initializer method for `Country`, but we also need to initialize `Country` within the initializer method of `City`, and this presents itself as a conundrum since `Country` depends on the initializer of `City` and `City` depends on the initializer of `Country`. To get a solution to this, you can declare the `capital` variable of `Country` as an implicit unwrapped optional property, which you denote by using `!`. This means that the `capital` property will have a default value as nil.

The `!` keyword also serves as a unwrapping function where you can get the value of the property without assigning that property to a local variable. As mentioned earlier, a variable that is denoted with the optional symbol, which is a `?` keyword, can either contain a value or nothing. So, when you are testing against this variable of the type denoted as optional, you need to know whether there is a value without directly accessing the underlying value. The `!` keyword means that you can unwrap the variable to get access to the value.

However, this does not absolve you from checking whether that property is nil as you still need to check for nil in your code.

So, now what happens is that `capital` has a default nil value and the `Country` instanced is considered as fully initialized as soon as the `Country` instance sets its `name` property within its own initializer method. This means that the `Country` initializer method can start to reference and pass around its `self` property as soon as the `name` property is set. So now the `Country` initializer can therefore pass the `self` property as one of the parameters for the `City` initializer when the `Country` initializer is setting its own `city` property.

Summary

As you can see, Swift is a big departure in terms of syntax, style, and paradigm from Objective-C. Swift was developed to move away from the C paradigm of programming where we need to wrap our heads around memory management, allocation, and deallocation. We went through some of the basic features of Swift and noted that Swift features more terse code, has made memory management, and is also fuss free, since ARC takes care of memory management for us in Swift. However, Swift is still in the beta stage at the time of this writing, so it can still be subject to changes in its journey to alpha and release status. Therefore, you can expect that some features will be added or removed during this period. However, the fundamentals of Swift will not be changed significantly, and I hope that this chapter has given you a better understanding of Swift and has prepared you for programming in Swift in the near future.

To find out more information about Swift, the best resource to refer to is Apple's website on Swift programming at `https://developer.apple.com/swift/blog/` as it has been updated constantly since Swift was announced.

In the next chapter, we will look at memory management techniques using some of the excellent tools in Xcode, such as Static Analyzer, and we will also cover more details on the various techniques so that you will know which debugging tool is the best tool to use in different situations.

9
Memory Management and Debugging

Back in the good old days of iOS 3 and previous versions, the management of computer memory was a laborious affair as every pointer and memory allocation needed to be tracked precisely, lest you experienced the dreaded situation of memory leaks due to a missing `release` keycode in your code and so on. However, with the release of iOS 4 and higher, Apple introduced ARC and developers all over the world rejoiced as they thought that the days of memory management were over. However, sadly, this is not the case as Objective-C is not like other programming languages such as Java or C#, where there is a garbage collector that will do the memory management and garbage collection for you. ARC only serves as an enabler to simplify memory management for us so that we do not need to explicitly call the `release` method such as `[myArray release]`, since ARC handles these for us. So while there are less brain cells that we need to allocate for memory management when developing an iOS app, we must still do some basic memory management even with the introduction of ARC, and this chapter will help you along the way with that. So to get things off the ground, here are the topics that we will cover in this chapter:

- Memory leaks
- Strong/weak references
- Retain cycles
- Memory overuse
- Using the debugger and breakpoints
- Collecting data on your AppPlumbing leaks
- Using the LLVM / Clang Static Analyzer
- Using NSZombie

Memory leaks

If you are used to calling the `release` method after an `alloc/init` method or a `retain` statement, ARC allows you to forgo all that as you can still call your `alloc/init` methods or `retain` statements and not add in a `release` statement as ARC takes care of this for you. This introduces brevity and makes your code more concise. Here is an example:

Before ARC:

```
Class1 *obj1 = [[Class1 alloc] init];
Class1 *obj2 = [obj1 retain];
[obj2 release];
[obj1 release];
```

After ARC:

```
Class1 *obj1 = [[Class1 alloc] init];
Class1 *obj2 = obj1;
```

If you wrote the code without calling the `release` methods as seen under *After ARC*, you will have two memory leaks that will appear in your code due to you forgetting to put in the two `release` methods. You will notice that the number of lines has been reduced and the code is easier to understand, as there is no need to call any `release` statements. So with ARC, people will be fooled into thinking that their memory management woes are over, but actually, memory leaks can still happen with ARC and I will show you how.

ARC helps in that it automates the addition of `retain/release/autorelease` statements to your code, but memory leaks can still occur with ARC. It is not so obvious to spot because people think that with ARC, there will not be any memory leaks. However, that is not the case and memory leaks can still occur with the presence of ARC, but there are some methods that you can use to find memory leaks. However, first, let's go through some terms.

Strong/weak references

A strong reference is synonymous with the `retain` property where you increment the reference count of an object by 1. In the world of ARC, the `retain` and `assign` properties are no longer used and are replaced with `strong` and `weak` respectively.

A `strong` reference is the default property of objects as it means that you want to get ownership of an object while a `weak` reference means that another object is holding ownership to the object you want and then you can't stop it from being deallocated since ownership does not belong to you.

The `strong` and `weak` references are denoted by the Objective-C `strong` and `weak` keyword respectively. Even with ARC, you can still have memory leaks appearing and some causes of memory leaks using ARC are:

- Retain cycles
- Creating secondary threads and not providing it with its own autorelease pool
- Using frameworks that have non-ARC code
- Referencing itself within a block, which creates a strong reference

Retain cycles

A retain cycle occurs when two objects such as a parent and child object have strong references to each other. A simple example would be the following code:

```
@interface MyParent : NSObject
@property (strong) MyChild *myChild;
@end

@interface MyChild : NSObject
@property (strong) MyParent *myParent;
@end
```

You can create an object of the type `MyParent` with the following code:

```
MyParent *myParent = [[MyParent alloc] init];
```

A retain cycle is created with the preceding line of code and here is how it looks:

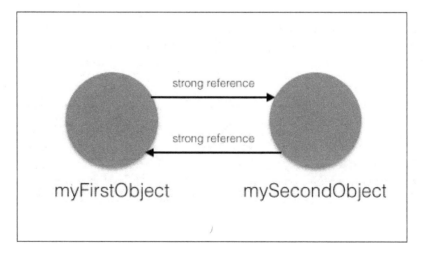

In the preceding diagram, you can quickly see what is called a retain cycle since **myParent** has a strong reference to **myChild**, and **myChild** has a strong reference to **myParent**. This is a form of memory leak where if an object tries to release an instance of the first object, it can't be released because the second object has a strong reference to the first object and a retain cycle is created. Do note that ARC will not fix all memory leaks for you, so you, the developer have to fix this type of memory leaks using some tools, which we will cover later on. As this type of memory leak is not very obvious, fixing it will require more effort and thinking, but thankfully, Apple has provided some tools that will aid us greatly in this.

A general rule of thumb to avoid a situation where a retain cycle can occur is to remember this—if object A wants to retain object B indefinitely, then object A has to be higher up in the hierarchy tree than object B, where object A has to have a strong reference to object B. If you have objects that are on the same level in the hierarchy tree, then you should put a weak reference to avoid a retain cycle. So in the preceding diagram, to avoid a retain cycles, `mySecondObject` should not have a strong reference to `myFirstObject`. However, if you do need to let `mySecondObject` have a reference to `myFirstObject`, then make it a weak reference instead of a strong reference. Tree hierarchies are safe and do remember that putting weak references will avoid a retain cycle and memory leaks.

Memory overuse

If you used enough iOS apps, you will notice that some apps will just force close themselves after you innocuously tap on a button or do some action. This is an iOS way of handling memory issues as it basically just says, "this app has a memory leak and you do not have enough memory to handle it, so this app has to be closed."

Altogether there are three memory warning levels for iOS. Level 1 and 2 will be displayed in your Xcode console when memory is running low, as shown in the following diagram. Level 3 occurs when your application crashes and goes back to Springboard, which is the term used to refer to the iOS home screen:

```
2014-04-13 14:17:32.641 MemoryManagement[87318:60b] Received
memory warning.
2014-04-13 14:17:39.799 MemoryManagement[87318:60b] Received
memory warning.
```

Using the debugger and breakpoints

One of the most fundamental debugging concepts of using an IDE, such as Xcode, is the concept of breakpoints, where you can stop your running program at a particular point in time as denoted by the breakpoint where your code is. Using the breakpoint is very simple; you just open up your Xcode project and click on the left side of the window where you code it and a blue indicator will appear, as shown here:

```
15   @implementation ViewController
16
17   - (void)viewDidLoad
18   {
19       [super viewDidLoad];
20
21       int catImageWidth = 254;
22       int catImageHeight = 198;
23
24       int count = 0;
25       //this will cause a spike i
26       while(true)
27       {
28           count++;
```

Next, when you run your application and when the program hits line number **26** at the `while(true)` statement, the program will halt and you can move your cursor over any variable before line number **26**, and Xcode will show you the value that the variable contains at that point in time. Breakpoints are useful in debugging memory leaks where you have an idea of where a leak appears and you want to see the value or memory address of that variable. You can put multiple breakpoints and use the Step Over command to step over each line of code to see how your program is executing. Here is a list of icons, that you will come across when debugging using breakpoints:

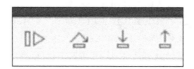

The four icons from the left to right in the preceding screenshot that you can use for breakpoint debugging are as follows:

Icons	Description
Continue program execution	This will let your program continue executing until it encounters the next breakpoint, or the program ends
Step Over	This will let your program execute the next line of code in the current scope
Step Into	This will let your program follow the method into its own code and view the code for the method
Step Out	This will take you out of the current context and into calling a method one step up into the program stack

Breakpoints are very useful for checking the values of your variables at a specific point in time when your program is halted due to the breakpoint and the four icons for breakpoint debugging will aid you in debugging memory-related and other logic bugs.

Collecting data on your app

Do note that a memory warning level does not necessarily mean that your application is leaking memory. There could be a situation where your application is loading or performing operations on large resources such as data files, images, videos, and so on and this will trigger the memory warning. ARC will handle the cleaning up later. However, if you see a memory warning level 2, then you should start to look at your code as the next memory warning level will be the actual application crash.

Debugging crashes and memory leaks are like the game of hide and seek or playing detective. There will be a lot of clues lying around, which will lead you to the culprit in your code that is causing a bothersome crash or memory leak. Apple has provided us with a lot of tools and logs, which will be useful for us in debugging our code. We will cover some of the commonly used methods here so that you can get cracking with regards to fixing those problems as soon as possible.

One of the easier ways is to plug your device into your machine via your cable, fire up Xcode, which will automatically detect your plugged-in device and then press *Shift + Command + C* to activate your debug console, which is a black screen on the bottom right of your Xcode screen. Or you can select **View | Debug Area | Activate Console** from your Xcode menu as shown here:

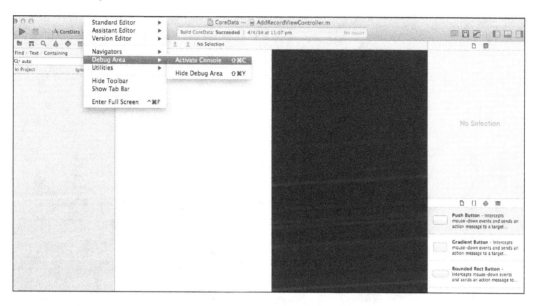

This will show all NSLog and crash output when you are running your app via a cable connection to Xcode.

However, there are occasions when you are testing your application, when it is not connected to your Xcode and it crashes at that moment. The preceding method does not work in this case, so what can you do? Do not fret, as there is another way to get your crash log once you are at your table and have plugged your iOS device into your machine and fired up Xcode.

Once you have started Xcode and plugged in your device where your app crashed, Xcode will actually be able to access your crash log on the device. To do so, all you need to do is click on the window and select **Organizer** from your Xcode menu, as shown in the following screenshot:

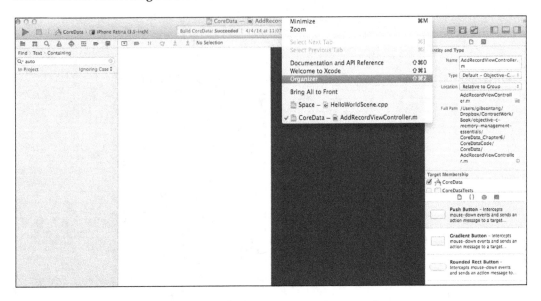

This will open your **Organizer**, which actually is a repository of all the devices that have been connected to Xcode and shows information such as the application's provisioning profile and screenshots. However, what we are really interested in is the crash logs.

So, click on the **Devices** button at the top and you will be shown all the developer information about all the devices that have connected to your device so far.

Click on your currently connected device, which is denoted by a green circle. Then, select the **Device Logs** option, which will then open another list of apps that have crashed. There you can sort the results by **Process**, which is the application name, **Type**, or **Date/Time**. Clicking on an item will reveal the crash log on the right side of the screen. There you can see the backtrace, which is actually a listing of all the methods that were called leading up to your crash. The last section of the code that caused your crash will be at the top of the backtrace, and you should start by looking from the bottom up to see how your app works and see all the functions and methods that it traversed through leading up to the crash:

```
Exception Type:  EXC_CRASH (SIGABRT)
Exception Codes: 0x0000000000000000, 0x0000000000000000
Triggered by Thread:  0

Last Exception Backtrace:
0   CoreFoundation              0x2e95be83 __exceptionPreprocess + 131
1   libobjc.A.dylib             0x30cbc6c7 objc_exception_throw + 38
2   CoreFoundation              0x2e95f7b7 -[NSObject(NSObject) doesNotRecognizeSelector:] + 202
3   CoreFoundation              0x2e95e0af ___forwarding___ + 706
4   CoreFoundation              0x2e8acdc8 _forwarding_prep_0___ + 24
5   CoreFoundation              0x2e91de71 __CFNOTIFICATIONCENTER_IS_CALLING_OUT_TO_AN_OBSERVER__ + 12
6   CoreFoundation              0x2e891ab1 _CFXNotificationPost + 1720
7   Bitissues                   0x0011762b 0x102000 + 87595
8   Bitissues                   0x001164f1 0x102000 + 83185
9   Bitissues                   0x0012a9c5 0x102000 + 166341
10  libdispatch.dylib           0x391a10c3 _dispatch_call_block_and_release + 10
11  libdispatch.dylib           0x391a10af _dispatch_client_callout + 22
12  libdispatch.dylib           0x391a39a9 _dispatch_main_queue_callback_4CF + 268
13  CoreFoundation              0x2e9265b1 __CFRUNLOOP_IS_SERVICING_THE_MAIN_DISPATCH_QUEUE__ + 8
14  CoreFoundation              0x2e924e7d __CFRunLoopRun + 1308
15  CoreFoundation              0x2e88f471 CFRunLoopRunSpecific + 524
16  CoreFoundation              0x2e88f253 CFRunLoopRunInMode + 106
17  GraphicsServices            0x335c32eb GSEventRunModal + 138
18  UIKit                       0x31144845 UIApplicationMain + 1136
19  Bitissues                   0x00108047 0x102000 + 24647
20  libdyld.dylib               0x391b5ab7 start + 2


Thread 0 Crashed:
0   libsystem_kernel.dylib      0x3926c1fc __pthread_kill + 8
1   libsystem_pthread.dylib     0x392d3a4f pthread_kill + 55
2   libsystem_c.dylib           0x3921d029 abort + 73
3   libc++abi.dylib             0x3866b98b abort_message + 71
```

Plumbing memory leaks

Next, we will look at a special tool present in Xcode to get in-depth information about your app while it is running. This special tool is actually a suite of tools that can perform the following functions:

- Examine and monitor one or more processes

- Record a sequence of user actions and replay them, just like a video recorder

- Save user interface recordings and then access them from Xcode

- This set of tools is known collectively as Instruments and they are more useful than NSLogs when tracking down difficult-to-reproduce bugs, such as random crashes and debugging memory leaks

- Analyze the performance of your app

- Perform stress testing on your app

- Gain a better understanding of how your application works

In this section, I will teach you the basics of Instruments and how to debug some code using it. So, to start off, you just need to follow these three simple steps:

1. Click the **Xcode** menu on the top left of your Xcode IDE.

2. Select **Open Developer Tool** from the list that appears.

3. A submenu will appear with the **Instruments** item, which you should click on:

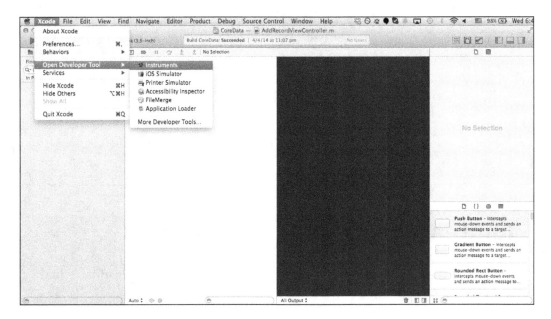

4. Then, you should see a pop-up window with the following options:

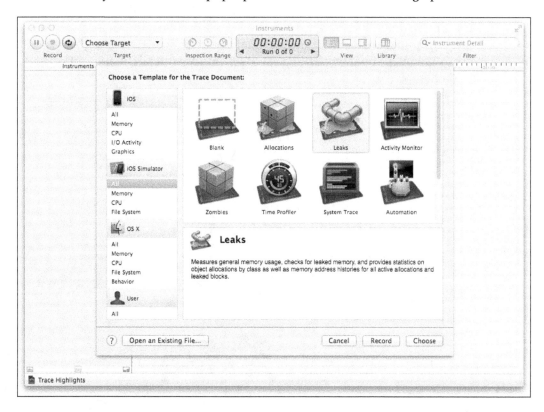

There are options such as **Leaks**, **Allocations**, and **Time Profiler**, which show all the various tools.

5. To have a little test run, open the `Instruments.xcodeproj` file, which has very leaky code and we will see how to use the Xcode debugging tool called **Instruments** to understand how the memory allocation spikes up when the code is running. So, to start things off, let's use the Xcode profiling tool to see our memory spike by clicking on the **Product | Profile** menu option as shown here:

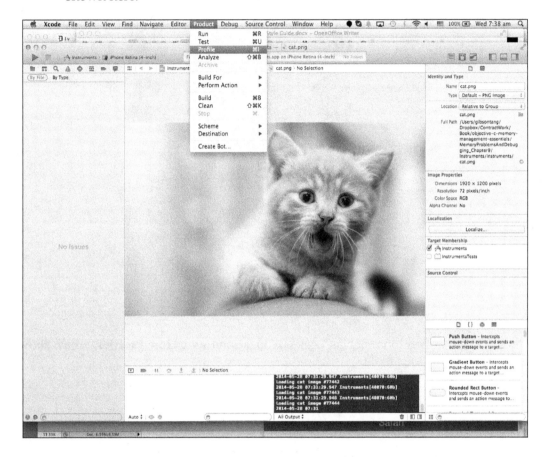

6. Then, Xcode will show the **Instruments** window and then you need to select **Allocations** options and click on the **Profile** button. Once you have clicked the **Profile** button, the leaky app will start executing and you will see the following screen. Keep an eye on the graph that you will see spiking up rapidly and also the **All Heap Allocations** row, which will show the amount of memory being consumed increasing in a very fast rate:

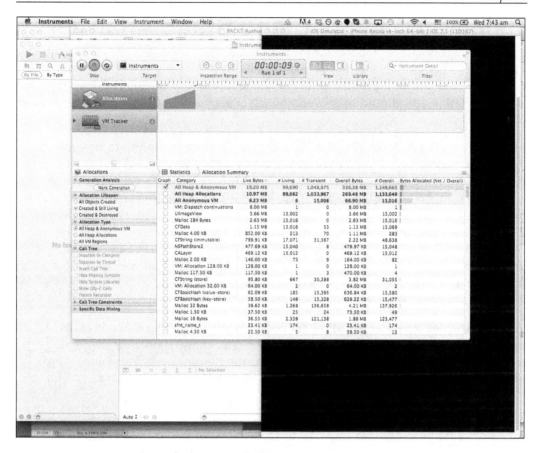

So, to reiterate the steps, we need to do the following:

1. Open Xcode.

2. Click on **Product | Profile**.

3. Click on **Allocations | Profile**.

4. Look at the **All Heap Allocations** section.

5. Look at the memory allocation on the graph.

6. Check for retain cycles or usages of itself within blocks that can hint or create a retain cycle.

Using the LLVM / Clang Static Analyzer

The Instruments suite of tools is meant to be used when your app is running. However, sometimes, as the saying goes, *an ounce of prevention is worth a pound of cure*. So, before you pull up Instruments to debug your app during runtime, there is a good step that you should follow and which is performing a static analysis on your code base.

Static analysis is a mechanism where a collection of algorithms and techniques are used to analyze your source code to find bugs. This may sound like what you do during the compilation stage, but there is an important difference. The act of compiling your code will tell Xcode to check your code base for syntax errors and flag out any errors or warnings that it detects. Static analysis goes one step deeper in that it analyzes your code to find potential bugs that will surface during runtime. Static analysis lets the program calculate all possible executions of a program, and the code is analyzed for quality, safety, and security so that you are alerted to bugs such as overflows, divide by zero, pointer errors, and so on. So, think of static analysis as runtime testing, but before your code has begun executing.

As static analysis goes deeper into your code, the amount of time Xcode takes to do the static analysis will be longer. So, use static analysis only for debugging hard-to-fix bugs or as a final step before submitting your app to the iTunes App Store. To activate static analysis of your app, click on **Product | Analyze** to let Xcode start its static analysis of your code:

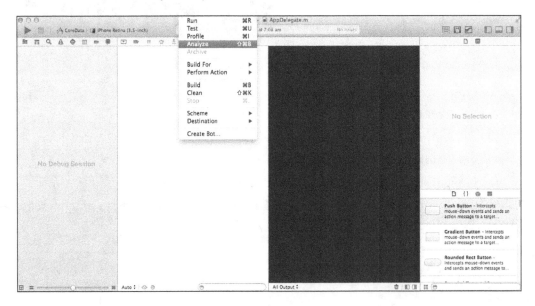

Depending on the size of your code base, static analysis can take seconds to even minutes while it dives deep into your code to ferret out any potential issues. A project that has only a few lines of code will take a few seconds to do the static analysis while a large project with thousands of lines of code will take a few minutes or more, depending on the size of the project. Then, click on the left side of your Xcode screen as shown in the preceding screenshot, to see the potential issues that Xcode found through static analysis.

By default, static analysis goes down to a deep level to analyze every corner of your code base. This consumes a lot of resources on your machine, and if you have a large code base or a slow machine, the amount of time used for static analysis can be quite big. Hence, you can adjust the level of static analysis that Xcode uses if you don't want an in-depth analysis, which may not find as many issues as a deep static analysis, but can still help surface some issues. Static analysis is useful as it can surface errors such as overflows, divide by zero, and so on, which a compiler can't detect. To change the level of static analysis, click on your project on the left, then select **Build Settings** and then look for the **Mode of analysis for 'Analyze'** option and set it to **Shallow (faster)** as shown here:

Using NSZombie

Last but not least, let me introduce you to the concept of NSZombie. NSZombie is a memory debugging aid that helps you in debugging memory leaks. As you may know, when an object has a retain count of 0, that object will be deallocated and not exist anymore. However, if you enable NSZombie, the object with a retain count of 0 will turn into a NSZombie instance instead. Then, when this NSZombie receives a message from another place in your code, it will show a warning instead of crashing your app or exhibiting unpredictable behavior.

NSZombie is useful for debugging subtle overrelease or autorelease bugs as these types of bugs tend to manifest itself in crashes or weird behavior. NSZombie will show these crashes and weird behavior as a warning instead, which will help in your debugging.

NSZombies exist in a strange half-alive/half-dead state as they are not deallocated when the retain count is 0, but they are not fully alive either. So, NSZombie is an apt term to use to describe these half-living/half-dead objects.

However, an important point to note is that NSZombies are to be disabled once you have finished debugging. NSZombies consume memory like any object with a retain count of 0, which is turned into NSZombie, which still occupies memory instead of being deallocated. So, if you do not disable NSZombie it will occupy more memory. In order to harness the power of NSZombie where it will log a warning instead of crashing your app or exhibiting unpredictable behavior, just follow these simple steps to activate NSZombie:

1. Click on the **Product** menu in your Xcode IDE.

2. Select the **Scheme** menu item.

3. Proceed to click on **Edit Scheme...** to open the popup to enable NSZombie:

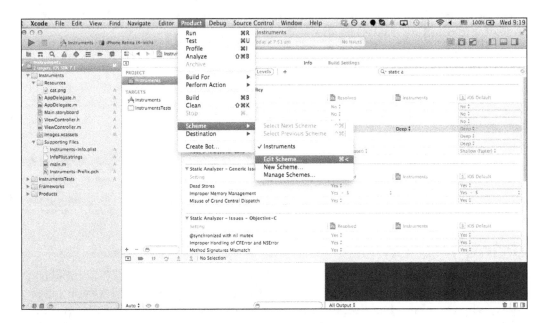

4. Then, you will see a popup appear with an **Enable Zombie Objects** option. Click on this checkbox and NSZombie will be enabled.

5. Finally, run your project and you will see NSZombie in action:

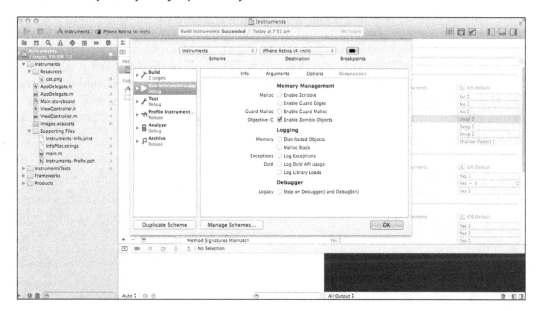

Finally, here is a table outlining which debugging tools should be used in which context so that you can use the right tool for the right situation:

Debugging tool	Appropriate context
Xcode Instruments	This is used to find memory leaks that cause crashes during runtime
Static Analyzer	This is used to analyze your code base for issues such as divide by 0, memory issues before the code is executed, and so on
NSZombie	This is used to show warnings instead of crashing due to memory leaks

Summary

We covered some aspects of the theory of memory management, such as retain cycles and strong/weak references. Then, we moved to the repercussions of memory leaks and the various warning levels. Following this, we discovered how to get crash logs to help you get information about your app and code. We then looked at a list of the various tools that Xcode possesses, such as Instruments and NSZombies, which will help us to debug memory leaks that can be caused by a myriad of causes, such as not releasing objects or releasing objects prematurely. Finally, we closed off with a description of static analysis and enabling NSZombies and their uses. With all these tools and information at your fingertips, I hope debugging memory leaks and errors have been made much easier for you since you have the tools required to make this a less painful journey.

In the next chapter, we will cover some developer tips for memory management, such as getters, setters, and other tips. So, let's head to the next chapter.

10
Tips and Tricks for Memory Management

Memory management is something that every programmer dealing with Objective-C will encounter although Apple introduces a lot of tools to assist in ferreting out memory-related issues such as Instruments and NSZombies. There are some more subtle techniques and tools that are present in Objective-C and Xcode, which we will be looking into in this chapter. Some are obvious and some will give you a new perspective with regards to Objective-C. We will also cover some important topics such as:

- Using the @property keyword
- Using the getter/setter methods
- Understand the property attribute in Objective-C
- When to avoid KVC and KVO

So, let's get started!

Objective-C, C, and memory management

Objective-C and the C programming language are closely related as Objective-C is a proper superset of C, which means that anything that works in C will work with Objective-C. So inherently, it also means that memory management methods and protocols that you are familiar with in C or C++ will also apply to Objective-C. However, a good thing about Objective-C is that the compiler does a lot of this memory management for you under the hood. This means that you do not need to write too much code to handle memory management in Objective-C compared to C or C++.

However, do note that although you can mix C++ and Objective-C together, Objective-C is not a superset of C++. This does not mean that you can be totally hands off with regards to memory management since Objective-C does not have a garbage collector like what you get in Java.

With the release of **Automatic Reference Counting (ARC)** support in Xcode 4.2 and iOS 4 and 5 onwards, developers everywhere thought that their days of laborious memory management are over, but make no mistake as you need to keep in mind that ARC is a compile time memory management mechanism, where the compiler will examine the source code and then add the `retain` and `release` messages into the compiled code. ARC is not the traditional garbage collection mechanism that Java and C# programmers are familiar with where garbage collection is done during runtime by the garbage collector.

So, the introduction of ARC means that there is even less typing for you as a developer as you do not need to type in `retain` and `release` messages explicitly into your code, which makes your code more verbose. However, as we saw in the previous chapters where we introduced retain cycles and other types of memory leaks, using ARC means that you will still need to be aware of memory management principles and that is where Objective-C and Xcode shines compared to their C programming language counterparts. Its built-in mechanism helps programmers avoid leaking memory through a series of good practices. So, let's start by looking at these good practices in detail in this chapter.

Getters and setters

If you have done some Java and C# programming and come from a Java or C# background, you should be familiar with getter and setter methods or you may also know them as accessors and mutators, respectively. They are a fundamental pillar of good programming. Getters/setters or accessors/mutators, are also known as methods used in keeping the principle of encapsulation where member variables are made private to protect them from other code which could be potentially malicious, and the getter/setter acts as a gatekeeper or intermediary between the private member variable and other code. Take a look at the following lines of code:

```
public int getAge()
{
  return Age;
}
public void setAge(int _age)
{
  Age = _age
}
```

The preceding two methods should not be unfamiliar to you from a Java or C# perspective. Getters and setters can be considered bad if used improperly. Making a variable public and yet writing a getter and setter method is a good example as this violates the concept of encapsulation. Now, getter and setter methods are a good foundation for recommended programming practices as they confer the following benefits and more:

- Hiding the internal state of the objects

- Setting different access levels such as read only, write only, and so on

- Creating a public interface will make it easier for you to make code changes when you need to change the implementation layer, which will be apparent when you need to make changes across many files

- Allowing you to enforce strict rules on what can be done and not be done with your objects via these getter and setter methods

Getter and setter methods generally start with the get and set prefix. This may come as a surprise to you, but Objective-C has very strong support for getter and setter methods. However, you may ask, "where are the getter and setter methods in Objective-C? I don't recall setting any methods or writing any code that start with get or set?" However, actually, they are present and are already in your code, but you just do not realize it yet since Objective-C has an abstraction layer for you so that you do not need to spend too much time writing getter and setter methods. This abstraction layer allows you to customize your getter and setter methods as we shall see later on. The way that Objective-C lets you define get and set methods and the various attributes such as readonly, readwrite, and so on is via the @property keyword in your code. Getters and setters go hand in hand with memory management as you can write code to clean up the memory in these methods if you need to.

The property attribute in Objective-C

If you have been doing some Objective-C programming, you would have come across the following syntax:

```
@property (nonatomic, readonly) UIView *rearView;
or
@property (nonatomic, retain) UIActivityIndicatorView
*loadingView;
```

Now, I would bet that you would generally have a foggy idea of what terms such as `nonatomic` or `retain` mean when you are assigning these properties such as `nonatomic` and so on to your objects. These keywords, such as `nonatomic` or `readonly`, actually define the properties of your objects, which are used in the getter and setter methods automatically created for you in Xcode. These terms are coding keywords related to memory management and access control and were not created just to baffle you or to give you additional typing to do (at least not as much typing as typing getter and setter methods themselves). Anyway, let's go through what these terms mean so that you will get a better understanding of these keywords in relation to getter and setters:

Attribute name	Description
nonatomic	This property is not thread safe, but it is faster than `atomic`.
atomic	This property is used for completeness and will not allow bad things to happen if a different thread tries to access this object at some point in your code. However, it is slower than `nonatomic` due to additional bookkeeping overhead required.
strong	This is used with ARC and helps by not letting you worry about the retain count of an object as it is autoreleased when you are done with it. In code that does not support ARC, it is a synonym for the retain property.
weak	This means that the reference count is not increased by 1, and it does not become an owner of an object, but it does hold a reference to it. This is just another term for `unsafe_unretained` for the non-ARC code.
assign	This property will generate a setter method, which will assign the value to the object instead of copying or retaining it.
copy	This is used for when the object is mutable where you create a copy of the object. Do note that copy cannot be used together with retain as the copy of the object will already have its retain count incremented by 1.
readonly	This property will make the object read-only and no setter method will be created in the `@implementation` section of the code.
readwrite	This means that the `read` and `write` attribute properties are applicable and the getter and setter methods are automatically created for you.

So, `@property(nonatomic, retain) NSString *text` will tell the compiler, "I have a member variable of the type NSString named text, so I will need a pair of getter/setter methods, which will use the retain/release procedure."

Now that you have defined the attributes of your member variables such as which one has `readonly`, which one has `readwrite`, and so on, what next?

Next, you will use the `@synthesize` keyword. The `@synthesize` keyword will tell the compiler, "Now that I have declared the property `nonatomic` and `retain` for my `NSString *text` object, please create the code now for the getter and setter pair of methods for my `NSString *text` object."

So, with just these two lines of code, we can tell Objective-C to create our getter and setter methods for us and assign properties such as read-only, write-only, and so on for our objects or variables. This is much better than typing in verbose getter and setter code as you would do in Java or C#.

Do note that `@synthesize` is automatically provided to you by default in Xcode 4.4 and onwards, but there may be cases where you need to add in the `@synthesize` keyword yourself explicitly, which we will go through later.

Now you know why `@synthesize` does what it does. `@property` and `@synthesize` helps to automate the creation of getter and setter methods along with ease of creation with regards to access rules and controls with only a few lines of code. The getter and setter methods do exist once you use `@property` and `@synthesize`, but you do not see them physically in your code as these methods do not show up in your code base, but you can actually have access to them.

Take a look at my property declaration here:

```
@property (nonatomic, readwrite) int myInt;

@synthesize myInt;
```

In your implementation file, you will find that the following code will compile perfectly fine, and this shows that _myInt is accessing the variable directly:

```
int yourInt = _myInt;
```

Once the variable is synthesized, an instance variable (or iVar for short) is automatically created and prefaced with an underscore. The presence of this underscore in a variable name is a naming convention to indicate that this is an iVar, and this is done automatically for you within Objective-C.

So, this is why there is no compiler error when you call _myInt as _myInt is automatically created for you by the compiler when you tell the compiler the properties of what myInt will do.

`@synthesize` will also create the validation rules, which you assign to a variable using your `@property` keyword. Validation rules such as `readonly` means that when you try to assign a value to your variable, you will get a compiler error **read only property cannot be reassigned**, and that is the validation rule of your automatically created setter (mutator) method at work without the writing of verbose code.

Let's look at some code, shall we? Let's create an object called `UserObject` and assign a variable call `Age` to it.

So, let's get started!

1. We begin by clicking on **File | New** or by pressing *Command + N* on your keyboard, and select **Cocoa Touch** and **Objective-C class**, as shown here:

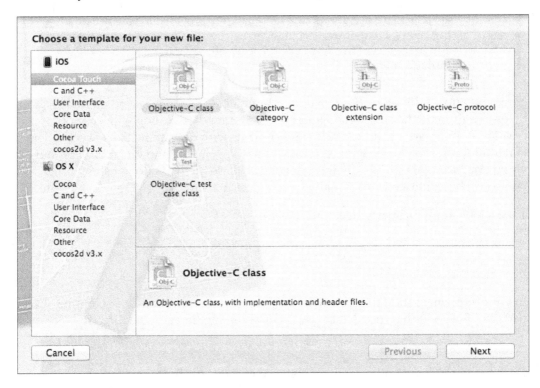

2. Next, we put in the name of the class, which is UserObject, and leave it as a subclass of NSObject:

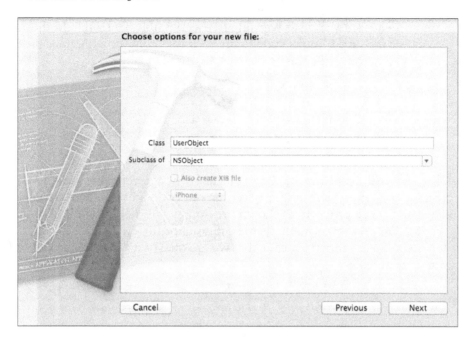

3. Then, click on **Next** followed by **Create** and your UserObject class will be created for you. Then, you should end up with this in your UserObject.h file. Add an integer called age and assign the nonatomic and readonly properties to it in your UserObject header file, as shown here:

```
#import <Foundation/Foundation.h>

@interface UserObject : NSObject
{
    int age;
}
@property (readwrite, nonatomic) int age;
@end
```

4. Now if you try to build your code, you will get a warning, **Autosynthesized property 'age' will use synthesized instance variable '_age', not existing instance variable 'age',** because you have not explicitly added in the code @synthesize age in the .m implementation file of your UserObject class.

This warning is just a friendly reminder that since you did not add in the `@synthesize age` code, Xcode will create an instance variable called `_age` for all your setter and getter methods. This is a harmless warning, but for me, I prefer to keep my code as warning free as possible, so I will add the `@synthesize age;` line of code to my `.m` implementation file of `UserObject` and get something like this:

```
@implementation UserObject

@synthesize age;//This is to remove the warning

@end
```

5. Next, we add `NSString *name` to our `UserObject` class and assign the `readwrite, nonatomic` property so that our code will now look as follows. The `readwrite` property as shown previously will tell the compiler that we want getter and setter methods to be automatically created for us and that the `nonatomic` property means that we are okay with the `age` variable being non-thread-safe:

```
@interface UserObject : NSObject
{
    int _age;
    NSString *name;
}

@property (readwrite, nonatomic) int age;
@property (readwrite, nonatomic) NSString *name;
@end
```

while our `.m` implementation file will look like this

```
#import "UserObject.h"

@implementation UserObject

@synthesize age, name;

@end
```

6. We can now create an instance of the `UserObject` class using `UserObject *user = [[UserObject alloc] init]`.

7. Next, we can see the magic of Xcode, where we put in the following code:

```
[user setName:"Joe"];
```

Notice that we did not create a getter or setter method for our NSString *name, but Xcode was smart enough to create it for us once we assigned the properties to NSString *name.

8. However, in some specific cases, you may want to override the default getter and setter methods that Xcode provides. Doing so is very easy, and using our int age as an example, we just create the following methods in our UserObject .h header file:

```
-(void) setAge:(int)aAge;
-(int) getAge;
```

9. We put in our custom getter and setter methods in our .m, UserObject implementation file as follows:

```
-(void) setAge:(int)aAge;
{
    int MIN_AGE = 20;//add in our validation logic for our
setter here
    if (aAge < MIN_AGE)
        age = 20;
    else
        age = aAge;
}

-(int) getAge
{
    return age;
}
```

So now, when you call the setAge method explicitly using the syntax such as [self setAge];, the code will call your custom setter method, since you have added your own getter and setter code to override the default getter and setter code that Xcode has created for you. This gives you efficiency and flexibility as Xcode will assume that you want the default getter and setter methods for your variables, and yet, you are free to override them if you need to which could occur in special cases.

Performance guidelines

Although iOS devices such as iPhones and iPads have a lot of memory compared to the early Nokia phones, it does not mean that you can be sloppy with regards to memory management. The iOS memory model and other mobile OSes do not include disk swap space, which are present on computer OSes, where persistent storage space is used as an extension of the memory space so that persistent storage can be used as a form of RAM for situations where low memory is encountered. So, the apps that you develop for iOS devices are more limited in the amount of memory that you can access.

Using large amounts of memory will lead to a serious degradation of system performance and triggering of the three memory warning levels, where the last warning level will lead to your application crashing. Plus, apps running under multitasking will share system memory with all other running apps that have higher priority such as the SMS application and phone application. So, you will never have 100 percent of the phone memory available for your application under any circumstance and even a brand new iOS device will have background processes running. So, reducing the amount of memory used by your iOS app should be a high priority task and not something that should be filed under a low priority tag.

If there is less free memory available in your device, that means the system will have a higher probability of being unable to fulfill future memory requests. If such a situation was to occur, the system will remove suspected apps and nonvolatile resources from memory. However, this is not a good solution as this is only temporary and those suspended apps and nonvolatile resources may be needed again a short while later.

The `UIViewController` class in `UIKit` in the iOS SDK provides useful ways to help you receive memory warnings in the console, which we saw in the previous chapters. I have listed three ways to implement memory warning notifications:

- You should implement the `applicationDidReceiveMemoryWarning` delegate method as this will be triggered when your application has some low memory warnings.

- To get a more granular memory warning such as `Received memory warning. Level=1` or `Received memory warning. Level=2` in your debug console, specifically for your `UIViewController`, you can implement the `didReceiveMemoryWarning` method of your custom `UIViewController` subclass.

- To get down to a class level, you can register your object to receive the
  UIApplicationDidReceiveMemoryWarningNotification notification
  via the addObserver method to call a specific method once the memory
  is running low, as shown here:

```
[[NSNotificationCenter defaultCenter] addObserver:self
selector:@selector(seeMemoryWarning:) name:
UIApplicationDidReceiveMemoryWarningNotification
object:nil];
- (void) seeMemoryWarning:(NSNotification *)notification
{
  NSLog(@"Low memory");
}
```

Once you see any of these warnings triggered in your code, you should respond
immediately by looking at how you can write the code to free up any unwanted
memory. A few ways to do this can be:

- Removing any views that are not visible to the user but are still loaded in
  memory by calling the removeFromSuperview method such as [myView
  removeFromSuperview];

- Releasing any images that are not on screen by setting them to nil

- Purging any data structures that are not used by your code at this point in
  time by calling the release method

Imagine that you have a memory leak in your application and the leak causing the
crash only appears after using the application for 2 hours. So, if you wish to replicate
the memory leak and trigger the crash in your code, you need to run the application
for 2 hours each time to see the crash. This can be a time consuming task as you
need to leave your app running, but thankfully, Xcode provides a way to trigger the
memory warning without actually producing a memory leak, and this feature comes
courtesy of the iOS simulator. You can click on **Hardware | Simulate Memory
Warning** in order to trigger a memory warning so that you can write and test your
memory cleanup code under the relevant memory warning method handler.

The following diagram shows where you need to click to trigger a memory warning:

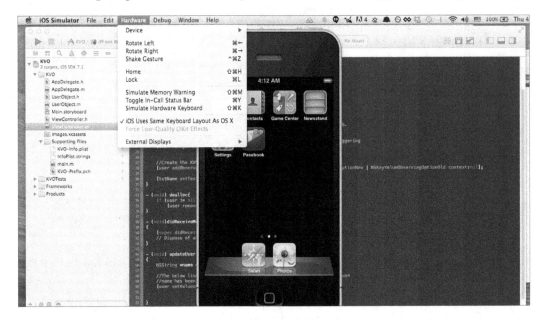

Doing so will allow you to test your iOS application under low memory conditions and then write the relevant code to reduce memory usage.

Don't overthink about memory management

Memory management is not something that is overly complex or difficult to wrap your head around. So, in order to further aid you with memory management, here are a few handy tips:

- You can try to make your resource files such as audio, images, and property lists as small as possible. To reduce the space occupied by property list files, you can use the NSPropertyListSerialization class while the free, open source command-line tool called Pngcrush can be used to compress PNG files as you can have savings of 20 percent or more depending on your PNG files.

- Core Data is more than just a persistent storage framework. Core Data provides a memory efficient way of managing large data sets, and if you manipulate large structured data, using the Core Data persistent store or SQLite database as a data store as opposed to NSData or NSUserDefault will ensure that you can have efficient memory usage provided by Apple's own Core Data framework.

- Resources should always be loaded when you need it, such as when you only need to see it on the device screen. This is called lazy loading, which we have seen in the previous chapter. You could be tempted to load all resources much in advance before you actually use it. However, this will actually mean that your resource is occupying memory when it is actually not being used at the current moment. So to optimize memory usage, always practice lazy loading.

- Finally, this is a little-known tip that you can use in your **Build Settings**: you can add the -mthumb compiler flag to help reduce the size of your code by using 16-bit instructions instead of 32-bit instructions, which uses up less space and this can result in savings of up to 35 percent. However, one caveat is that if your iOS application floating point intensive code and your application needs to support ARMv6 such as older generation iPod Touches and older iPhones, then the -mthumb option should not be used for your application. However, if your code is for ARMv7, then you can enable the -mthumb option in your Xcode project, which is enabled by default.

When to avoid KVC and KVO

KVC and KVO, which we covered previously in *Chapter 7, Key-value Programming Approaches*, seems like a great mechanism for notifications at a very granular level, but it is possible to go wrong with KVO if you use it incorrectly. The removeObserver method will crash if you are not the observer for that key path, so keeping an exact track of the properties that you are observing is a must.

KVO only has one callback method. If you have multiple notifications, you need to handle them within one callback method, which makes your code inelegant and clunky like this:

```
- (void)observeValueForKeyPath:(NSString *)keyPath
ofObject:(id)object change:(NSDictionary *)change context:(void
*)context {
  if ([keyPath isEqualToString:@"mySize"])
  {
          //Do something else
      }
  else if ([keyPath isEqualToString:@"anotherSize"])
  {
    //Do something else
  }
}
```

With a few more notifications, you will write a lot of if-else statements and you will be able to see how unwieldy the code will be and many bad things such as crashes, bugs, and so on will appear, and this requires more debugging time.

KVO registering can crash your app if you do it multiple times. If you have a superclass that is observing the same parameter on the same object, the `removeObserver` method will be called twice and it would lead to a crash on the second time.

KVO works in a wonderful and magical way in the same way as callbacks. Code utilizing callback can be painful to debug. So, I would recommend KVO usage if you have adequate experience with KVO and start with small projects as the API documentation is sparse and it can lead to debugging problems down the road if you are not well versed with KVO.

Summary

Finally, we reached the end of this chapter. This chapter covers some details of Objective-C, such as property attributes, which you have been typing in but do not have a clear idea of. We also covered memory management guidelines, where I have outlined some tips and tricks to add to your knowledge of memory management and debugging memory-related issues in your code. This chapter just covers a small subset of memory management and I hope that you have dived deep into the previous chapters, where the various memory management techniques are covered more in-depth. Finally, one more chapter lies ahead, where we will go through some of the new tools and functionalities of Xcode 6, which you can use in your projects. So, let's proceed, shall we?

11
Features of Xcode 6

In this final chapter, we will go in-depth into the de facto **Integrate Development Environment (IDE)** provided by Apple, which is used by developers to create iOS and Mac OS applications.

We will cover the following topics in this chapter:

- Introduction to Xcode 6
- What's new in storyboard?
- Debugging in Xcode 6
- An Interface Builder in Xcode 6
- Exploring playground

Introducing Xcode 6

Xcode 6 was announced by Apple at the **Worldwide Developers Conference (WWDC)** on June 2, 2014 and it was officially released on September 17, 2014. Xcode 6 improved a lot with regards to features and tools for iOS and Mac developers as it has support for the new Swift programming language created by Apple and announced in 2014.

Xcode 6 also includes new features such as live rendering within Interface Builder where your handwritten UI code is displayed within the UI canvas and any change is also instantly reflected when you type in your code. It also has a new view debugging tool that you can use to help you see your UI layers in a 3D visualization so that you can understand the composition of your interface and see and identify any clipped or overlapped views.

With Apple releasing newer devices every year with different screen sizes, having to support multiple screen devices is not an easy task to do. However, Xcode 6 now has new features that are aimed at reducing the tedium of developing iOS apps for multiple screens. So, let's dig into this chapter and look at the new tools that Apple has provided for us.

In this entire chapter, we will devote the following paragraphs to examining the internals and new features that are present in Xcode 6.

What's new in storyboard

Xcode 6 introduces a few new features with regards to storyboards and Interface Builder. Ever since the introduction of Xcode 4, storyboard allows you to link up your screen using a visual interface, describe the transition between the various screens, and have a good conceptual overview of all the screens since they are all placed into a single file. Storyboards have been an important tool for programmers, developers, and designers to create interfaces easily and link them up using a GUI. This is especially useful for designers as it allows them to overcome their fear of writing code, and storyboard allows them to create intuitive interfaces easily.

Similarly, with the introduction of Xcode 6, there have been new additions and changes to Storyboard. A few of the new additions are:

- Allowing storyboard or the NIB file to replace launch images
- Universal storyboard

Now, let's expand more on the two new features in Xcode 6, which I mentioned earlier.

Allowing storyboard or the NIB file to replace launch images

When an iOS application is busy loading its initial first screen, the iOS (operating system) will show a static image, which is inserted into the application by the app developer. For an optimal effect, the launch image should resemble the user interface of the application. More information about launch images can be found on Apple's website at `https://developer.apple.com/library/ios/documentation/userexperience/conceptual/mobilehig/LaunchImages.html`, where it mentions this:

"A launch file or image provides a simple placeholder image that iOS displays when your app starts up. The placeholder image gives users the impression that your app is fast and responsive because it appears instantly and is quickly replaced by the first screen of your app. Every app must supply a launch file or at least one static image.

In iOS 8 and later, you can create a XIB or storyboard file instead of a static launch image. When you create a launch file in Interface Builder, you use size classes to define different layouts for different display environments and you use Auto Layout to make minor adjustments. Using size classes and Auto Layout means that you can create a single launch file that looks good on all devices and display environments."

Before iOS 8 and Xcode 6, developers had to provide launch images for each screen size, which can cover iPad, iPhones 4S, iPhone 5S, and so on. If your application is a universal application, that means you need to provide multiple versions of the launch images to support the various devices. But now with the introduction of using storyboards as launch images, you can use Auto Layout to create a single launch storyboard and this launch storyboard can be used as the launch image of all the devices that you are supporting. This is a very handy time-saving methods as this means that you do not need to create multiple launch images for various screen sizes anymore.

So, in the next few pages, we will go through a short introduction to using storyboards as launch images and you will appreciate this additional functionality that has been added into Xcode 6 for the sake of all developers. Do note that this function only works on iOS 8 and not on iOS 7. So, if you are targeting devices using iOS 7, then using storyboards as launch images will not work for you and you need to revert back to the old method of using static images. However, considering this, most iOS users tend to upgrade their OS whenever a new version is released. From now on, you should be using storyboards as launch images often. However, do keep in mind that if you need to support iOS 7, you can use launch images as a fallback for devices running iOS 7, and yet use launch storyboards for devices running iOS 8. So, let's get going and I will walk you through this new nifty feature available in Xcode 6.

Launching images from your app

For this section, we will create a simple app to load a storyboard as a launch image. So, let's start, shall we?

1. First, we will create our project. For this tutorial, we will use a single view application after selecting **File | New Project**:

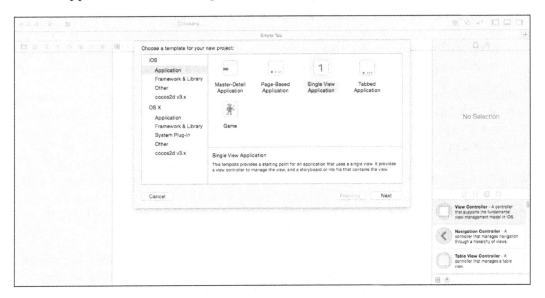

You will also see the following screen:

Then, we need to create a storyboard that will be the first image that the user sees when they launch the app, so we need to create a new storyboard and call it `launch.storyboard`. Do note that we need to add a view controller and can add other controls such as UILabels to our launch storyboard:

2. Next, we need to click on our project, which is named **LaunchApplication** and then set the **Launch Screen File** option to `launch.storyboard`, which is the storyboard that we just created:

3. To verify, we can go to `info.plist` and look for this key: **Launch screen interface file**. If this key exists, it means the value that is mapped to this key is the name of the storyboard or NIB file that we are using for our launch image:

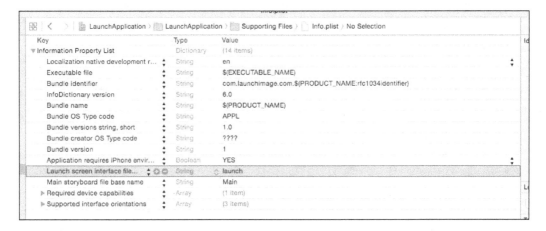

4. Then, we need to go to our `launch.storyboard` file and then select our **View Controller** for the `launch.storyboard` file and then click on the attributes inspector icon and make sure that **Is Initial View Controller** is checked.

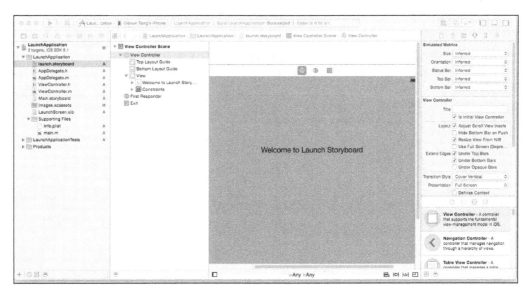

5. Finally, we need to build the project and run it to see that the launch image is now showing the `launch.storyboard` file, which has the text **Welcome to Launch Storyboard**:

With just a few steps, we are able to use a storyboard or NIB file to replace our launch images, PNGs, and with the help of Auto Layout, replacing multiple launch images with just one storyboard or NIB is made easy in just a few steps.

With just these simple steps, we can use a launch storyboard.

Universal storyboards

Now, let's move on to the next cool feature of Xcode 6 and that is universal storyboard. Universal storyboards means that your storyboard will be able to display the UI elements such as `UITextfields` and `UIButtons` in the correct position regardless of whether it is viewed with and iPad, iPhone 6+, and so on. So, you can create one storyboard and use it for iPad, iPhones, and other devices. The universal applications, which are applications that can be downloaded once and then run equally well on iPhones and iPads, are now becoming the norm in the iTunes App Store. There used to be the issue of generating different set of layouts for iPhone, iPads, retina devices, and non-retina devices. However, with the introduction of Auto Layout, it has made life easier for developers everywhere and Xcode 6 has made it easier for us with the addition of universal storyboards. With universal storyboards, Xcode 6 now allows us to easily see how our layouts will look with devices of different resolution after we have used Auto Layout to create the user interface layout.

To activate universal storyboards, we just need a few simple steps and use our Xcode project created to launch images to show you the simple steps we need. Do note that this feature will only work on iOS 8.

First, we need to select our **View Controller** in `Main.storyboard` and click the file inspector icon on the right of our screen and then make sure that **Use Size Classes** is checked:

Next, you will notice that at the bottom of your storyboard, there is an icon that you can click, which you can drag and resize to simulate how your Auto Layout user interface will look based on various screen layouts such as iPad portrait, iPhone landscape, and so on. So, feel free to click on it and move it around to see how your layouts will look and then adjust it according to your preference and specifications:

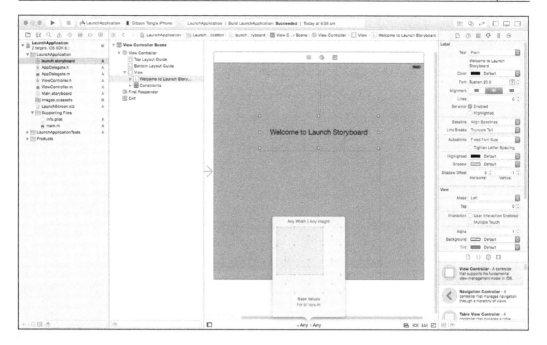

Debugging in Xcode 6

As you can see, Xcode 6 has added some nifty new tools for us, developers, to aid us in our work. However, not only this, debugging is easier now with some additional goodies that are now part of Xcode 6. Here are a few of the debugging goodies that are provided:

- View hierarchy debugger
- Debug gauges
- Enhanced queue debugging

Out of the list of additional debugging goodies, the view hierarchy debugger is the one that will prove most useful in terms of impact. Prior to Xcode 6, if you wanted to see the view hierarchy of your application, you had to use plugins such as Spark Inspector, Reveal, and so on. However, with the release of Xcode 6, view hierarchy visualization is now officially supported and you will get the full power of the view hierarchy in Xcode 6.

To use the view hierarchy debugger in Xcode 6, you need to make sure that your application is currently running, then you need to click the debug view hierarchy icon at the bottom of your, Xcode as shown, here and the button will have mouseover text called **Debug View Hierarchy** when you move over the icon:

When you click on that icon, you will see a spinning **UIActivityIndicator** appear for a few seconds before an image of your current view appears. Then you can just drag up, down, left, and right to rotate your view along a 3D axis to see the image they lines up, as shown here:

The view hierarchy debugger will have a few options, as shown here, which you can use to aid your debugging:

Starting from left to right, the following table shows what the various buttons do:

Icon	Button name	Functionality
	Show clipped content	This hides or shows content that is clipped
	Show constraints	This shows the Auto Layout constraints
	Reset viewing area	This resets the view to the default state
	Adjust view mode	This shows the view as wireframe, with contents
	Zoom out, actual size and zoom in	This sets the scale of the view

Debug gauges

Debug gauges has been spruced up with two new gauges and they are:

- The network activity gauge
- The disk activity gauge

The network activity gauge will show you how much data is being sent and received alongside a list of open ports and the details such as IP address, as we can see in the following screenshot. The typical scenario when you will use this network activity gauge is when you need to track the amount of data being sent and received if you need to do network optimization, plus see the remote IP address and port number so that you can have an idea of where the device is connecting to.

These will be useful if you want to minimize the amount of network traffic being sent and using the network activity gauge will be the first place you should look:

The disk activity debug gauge will show real-time data of all the reads and writes that your application is doing to disk. It also gives information on all open files coupled with a log of the disk I/O activity for you to look at, which you can see in the following screenshot. If you are developing applications that do large read and writes to disk and are experiencing erratic disk read and write failures, this disk activity debug gauge will be a enormous boon to you as it will tell you the size of the read and write activities. This is a great tool for you so that you can use these figures to track how much data you are actually reading and writing to disk, which will in turn help you to get a better picture of your situation in order to fix your problems:

What's new in Interface Builder

Interface Builder has few functions that are new in Xcode 6 and they are:

- Live rendering
- Size classes
- Preview assistant

Live rendering functions in exactly the same way as its name suggests. So, what live rendering does is display and render custom objects such as custom buttons, fonts, and so on in your Xcode IDE without building a line of code. So, what this means is that when you update your code for your custom objects, the Interface Builder design canvas will automatically update itself with the new look that you have just entered in the editor without requiring you to build and run your project to see it on the simulator or device. Previously, you had to run your app to see the changes that you did to custom objects, which are elements such as UIButtons, fonts, and so on that you created in storyboard or programmatically and which have a customized look to them. However, now, Apple has made it easier for us by introducing live rendering into Xcode 6 as it saves us time for development by not letting us waste time in building and running our code to see custom objects during the course of your development. You can expect to build and run your code thousands or even millions of times, so every second saved doing unnecessary building will save you hours of development time down the line.

One last thing that is new in Xcode 6 is the concept of size classes; we briefly covered size classes earlier on when I introduced the concept of universal storyboards. To explain in more detail, size classes for iOS 8 enables a developer to create and design a single universal storyboard with customized layouts for both iPad and iPhone. With the introduction of size classes, you can define common views and constraints once and then add your own custom variations for each supported device screen and form factor.

Finally, one more exciting feature in Xcode 6 is the preview assistant. The preview assistant allows you to preview and see how your layout looks one beside the other in different devices/targets. So, you can see your layout as it will appear on an iPad or iPhone 4S next to each other. To activate preview assistant, you need to click on the **Show Assistant Editor** button on the top right to activate Assistant Editor, then when Assistant Editor appears, click on the icon with the two interlinked icons, which will reveal a menu item called **Preview**. Click on the **Preview** item and select the storyboard that you wish to preview as shown here:

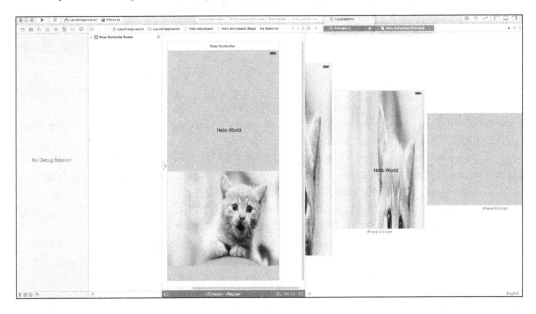

Next, you can see a **+** icon in the bottom-left corner. Click on it and you will see a list of iOS devices for different screen sizes, such as iPhone 4 inch, iPhone 4.7 inch, and so on.

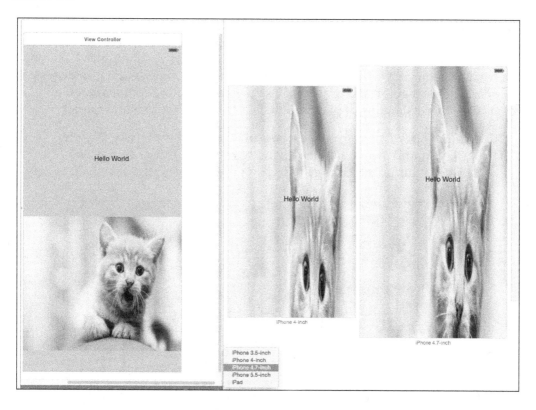

These correspond to the various iOS screen devices that you wish to preview. So, click on a device and a canvas showing that screen size will appear, and in that canvas, you can see how your selected storyboard looks for that screen size. So, without building and selecting your targeted simulator, Xcode 6 allows you to preview how your layout looks without wasting a few seconds of build time. This features well for storyboard and XIB files too. To sum up, the steps to use preview assistant are as follows:

1. Click on **Show Assistant Editor** on the top right to activate Assistant Editor.

2. Click on the icon with the two interlinked icons to reveal a menu called **Preview**.

3. Click on the **Preview** item and select the storyboard you wish to preview.

4. Click on the **+** icon in the bottom-left corner to select a list of iOS devices to see how your storyboard will look in that selected device screen.

Playground for Swift

Apple announced the programming language Swift in 2014 during WWDC and in line with that, Xcode 6 comes with a new feature called Playground where you can have an interactive work area to write Swift code and get live feedback in Xcode. This makes writing Swift code simple and fun as you can input in a single line of code and see the results immediately. And if your code iterates through a loop, you can see its movement via the timeline assistant. The timeline assistant also displays your variables in a graph and draws each step when a view is composed. To give you a better understanding of playground, let's try it out via a simple project:

1. To start off, we need to create a new playground by selecting the **File | New | Playground** menu and then giving our playground a name as you can see here. For this project, let's call our playground project `MyPlayground`:

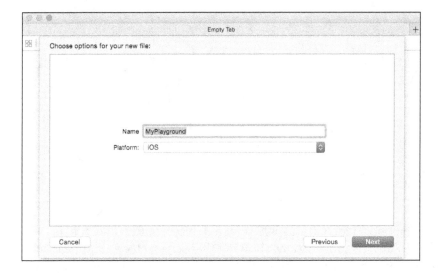

2. Next, a screen will appear where you can enter Swift code and the results will be shown instantly on the right side. To test it, try entering the following code:

```
import UIKit

var str = "Hello, playground"
var name = "Gib"

var sum = 0
for i in 0...10
{
```

```
        sum += i
    }

    sum
```

3. Next, you will see the results of your Swift input on the right side of the screen, which you can see here:

Now, that looks pretty cool as the real-time feedback helps by telling you what the output is and provides validation of your code. This can be useful for developers who want to test an algorithm without building their code or for you to display drawing code and see it immediately.

Although playground sounds good, there are some limitations that you have to note for playground. Here is a list of limitations of what cannot be done with playground:

- It cannot be used for user interaction
- Playground only works on the simulator and not on the device
- Customer libraries and frameworks cannot be imported as only system libraries and frameworks can be used

Summary

As you can see, Xcode is a big step forward in the right direction for developers with the introduction of new tools such as view hierarchy debugger, preview editor, and the addition of new functionalities such as allowing storyboards and NIBs to be used as launch images for your application instead of just static images. With all these new components to play with, Apple has made it much easier and better for developers to create and code cool projects with ease and reduce the effort to do so. With this, I leave you to your coding tasks and hope that you have a great time reading this book and getting some useful tips. With this, I bid you, "Goodbye, and enjoy coding."

P.S. If you wish to dig more into Xcode 6, here is a link to the official Apple documentation for Xcode 6: `https://developer.apple.com/library/ios/documentation/DeveloperTools/Conceptual/WhatsNewXcode/Articles/xcode_6_0.html`.

Index

Symbols

A

B

C

key-value observing (KVO)
  about 100
  implementing 100-103
  performance considerations 103
  avoiding 153

L

lazy loading 59, 60
live rendering functions 167
LLVM/ Clang Static Analyzer
  using 136, 137

M

Manual Reference Counting (MRC) 13
Manual Retain Release (MRR) 1
memory leak
  about 6, 124
  memory overuse 126
  plumbing 131-135
  retain cycle 125, 126
  strong reference 124, 125
  weak reference 124
memory management
  about 141, 152
  C 141
  data, collecting on app 128-130
  memory leaks 124
  Objective-C 141
memory management, Swift 117-120
memory model, Objective-C 19
memory warning notifications
  implementing 150, 151
Model-View-Controller (MVC) 68

N

network activity gauge 165
NSBinaryStoreType 73
NSException class 30
NSFetchRequest class 74
NSInMemoryStoreType 73

NSKeyValueCoding protocol
  about 92
  custom lookup path, advantages 96
  custom lookup path, disadvantages 96
  manual subsets 95, 96
NSManagedObject class 74
NSManagedObjectContext class 74
NSObject
  about 6-10
  class 8
  protocol 8
NSPersistentStoreCoordinator class 74
NSPredicate class 74
NSProxy 8
NSRunLoop class 29, 30
NSSQLiteStoreType 73
NSXMLStoreType 73
NSZombie
  about 139
  using 137-139

O

Objective-C
  about 105, 106, 141
  memory management 2
  memory model 19, 20
  objects 6
  programmer responsibility 49
  property attribute 143-149
object ownership
  about 2, 3
  life cycle 2, 3
  reference counting 4, 5
Object-relational mapper (ORM) 73
objects
  creating 35, 36
  immutability 42, 43
  initializing 35, 36
  mutability 43, 44
  serialization 65

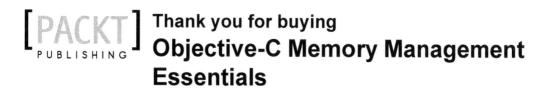

Thank you for buying
Objective-C Memory Management Essentials

About Packt Publishing

Packt, pronounced 'packed', published its first book, *Mastering phpMyAdmin for Effective MySQL Management*, in April 2004, and subsequently continued to specialize in publishing highly focused books on specific technologies and solutions.

Our books and publications share the experiences of your fellow IT professionals in adapting and customizing today's systems, applications, and frameworks. Our solution-based books give you the knowledge and power to customize the software and technologies you're using to get the job done. Packt books are more specific and less general than the IT books you have seen in the past. Our unique business model allows us to bring you more focused information, giving you more of what you need to know, and less of what you don't.

Packt is a modern yet unique publishing company that focuses on producing quality, cutting-edge books for communities of developers, administrators, and newbies alike. For more information, please visit our website at www.packtpub.com.

Writing for Packt

We welcome all inquiries from people who are interested in authoring. Book proposals should be sent to author@packtpub.com. If your book idea is still at an early stage and you would like to discuss it first before writing a formal book proposal, then please contact us; one of our commissioning editors will get in touch with you.

We're not just looking for published authors; if you have strong technical skills but no writing experience, our experienced editors can help you develop a writing career, or simply get some additional reward for your expertise.

iOS 7 Game Development

ISBN: 978-1-78355-157-6   Paperback: 120 pages

Develop powerful, engaging games with ready-to-use utilities from Sprite Kit

1. Pen your own endless runner game using Apple's new Sprite Kit framework.

2. Enhance your user experience with easy-to-use animations and particle effects using Xcode 5.

3. Utilize particle systems and create custom particle effects.

Application Development in iOS 7

ISBN: 978-1-78355-031-9   Paperback: 126 pages

Learn how to build an entire real-world application using all of iOS 7's new features

1. Get acquainted with the new features of iOS7 through real-world, project-based learning.

2. Take an in-depth look at Xcode 5, Foundation, and autolayout.

3. Utilize the full source code and assets present to build an actual interactive application.

Please check **www.PacktPub.com** for information on our titles

iOS Development with Xamarin Cookbook

ISBN: 978-1-84969-892-4   Paperback: 386 pages

Over 100 exciting recipes to help you develop iOS applications with Xamarin

1. Explore the new features of Xamarin and learn how to use them.

2. Step-by-step recipes give you everything you need to get developing with Xamarin.

3. Full of useful tips and best practices on creating iOS applications.

Xamarin Mobile Application Development for iOS

ISBN: 978-1-78355-918-3   Paperback: 222 pages

If you know C# and have an iOS device, learn to use one language for multiple devices with Xamarin

1. A clear and concise look at how to create your own apps building on what you already know of C#.

2. Create advanced and elegant apps by yourself.

3. Ensure that the majority of your code can also be used with Android and Windows Mobile 8 devices.

www.ingramcontent.com/pod-product-compliance
Lightning Source LLC
LaVergne TN
LVHW062316060326
832902LV00013B/2256